I0625171

Self-awareness

Unlock Your True Potential: The Comprehensive Guide to Mastering Self-Awareness and Living a Fulfilling Life in the Modern World - A Practical and Inspirational Self-Help Book for Personal Growth and Transformation

Lance P. Richards

Self-awareness: Unlock Your True Potential: The Comprehensive Guide to Mastering Self-Awareness and Living a Fulfilling Life in the Modern World - A Practical and Inspirational Self-Help Book for Personal Growth and Transformation

Table of Contents

01: Introduction to Self-Awareness: The Foundation of Personal Growth

Self-awareness is the foundation upon which personal growth and transformation are built. It is the ability to observe oneself and understand one's thoughts, feelings, and behaviors. This ability to reflect on oneself is essential to developing a deeper understanding of who we are, what we want, and how we can become the best version of ourselves.

The modern world is filled with distractions, and it is easy to become disconnected from our inner selves. Many people find themselves going through the motions of life without ever stopping to ask themselves what they truly want or who they want to be. They may be successful in their careers, but they still feel unfulfilled and disconnected from their true selves.

The good news is that self-awareness is a skill that can be developed, and it is never too late to start the journey of self-discovery. Through this journey, you will learn to understand yourself better, identify your strengths and weaknesses, and gain clarity on your goals and aspirations. You will also develop greater empathy and understanding of others, which can enhance your personal and professional relationships.

This book is a comprehensive guide to mastering self-awareness and living a fulfilling life in the modern world. It is a practical and inspirational self-help book for personal growth and transformation. It is designed to help you develop the skills you need to become more self-aware, so you can live a more fulfilling and meaningful life.

In the following chapters, we will explore the different aspects of self-awareness and provide practical tools and exercises to help you develop your self-awareness skills. We will also explore how self-awareness can help you achieve greater success in your personal and professional life, and how it can enhance your relationships with others.

But before we delve into the specifics of self-awareness, let us first take a closer look at what self-awareness is and why it is so important.

Self-awareness is the ability to observe oneself without judgment. It is the ability to reflect on one's thoughts, feelings, and behaviors, and to understand how they impact oneself and others. Self-awareness involves being honest with oneself about one's strengths and weaknesses, and being willing to take responsibility for one's actions.

Why is self-awareness so important? For one, self-awareness is the foundation of personal growth. It is impossible to grow and change if you are not aware of your own thoughts, feelings, and behaviors. Self-awareness is also essential to making good decisions. When you are aware of your own biases, fears, and limiting beliefs, you are better able to make decisions that are aligned with your values and goals.

Self-awareness is also critical to building healthy relationships. When you are aware of your own emotions and reactions, you are better able to communicate effectively with others. You are also more likely to be empathetic and understanding of others, which can enhance your personal and professional relationships.

In summary, self-awareness is the foundation of personal growth and development. It is essential to developing a deeper understanding of oneself, making good decisions, and building healthy relationships. In the following chapters, we will explore the different aspects of self-awareness and provide practical tools and exercises to help you develop your self-awareness skills. Let us begin the journey to self-discovery and personal transformation.

02: Understanding Self-Awareness: The Key to Unlocking Your True Potential

Introduction:

The concept of self-awareness has been around for centuries, and it is an essential aspect of personal growth and development. It is the ability to understand oneself, one's thoughts, emotions, and behaviors, and how they influence our lives. Self-awareness is the foundation for self-improvement and personal transformation. In this chapter, we will explore the meaning of self-awareness, its importance in our lives, and how we can develop it to unlock our true potential.

What is Self-Awareness?

Self-awareness is the ability to introspect and understand oneself. It is the conscious knowledge of one's own character, emotions, and motives. It is the process of examining our thoughts, feelings, and actions, and being able to recognize patterns in our behavior. It is a critical element of emotional intelligence, which is the ability to recognize and manage one's emotions effectively.

02: UNDERSTANDING SELF-AWARENESS: THE KEY TO UNLOCKING YOUR TRUE POTENTIAL

The Importance of Self-Awareness:

Self-awareness is essential for personal growth and development. It helps us to understand ourselves better, our strengths, weaknesses, and limitations. It allows us to identify and manage our emotions effectively and to develop healthy relationships with others. Self-awareness is the key to unlocking our true potential and living a fulfilling life.

The Benefits of Self-Awareness:

Self-awareness has numerous benefits for our lives. Firstly, it helps us to develop a better understanding of ourselves, our thoughts, and emotions. This knowledge allows us to make better decisions, set realistic goals, and prioritize our values. Secondly, self-awareness helps us to improve our relationships with others. When we are aware of our emotions and behaviors, we can communicate more effectively and empathize with others. Thirdly, self-awareness allows us to manage stress and anxiety better. When we understand our triggers and patterns of behavior, we can take steps to prevent or manage them. Finally, self-awareness enables us to develop resilience and adaptability. By understanding ourselves, we can learn from our experiences and grow as individuals.

How to Develop Self-Awareness:

Developing self-awareness is a lifelong process, but there are several ways to start. Firstly, we can start by examining our thoughts and emotions regularly. We can do this by journaling or simply taking a few minutes each day to reflect on our experiences. Secondly, we can seek feedback from others. Asking for feedback from trusted friends, family members, or colleagues can help us gain a different perspective on ourselves. Thirdly, we can practice mindfulness. Mindfulness involves being present in the moment and observing our thoughts and emotions without judgment. It can help us become more aware of our patterns of behavior and develop a more compassionate approach to ourselves. Fourthly, we can seek professional help. Working with a therapist or coach can provide us with valuable insights and tools to develop our self-awareness.

Conclusion:

Self-awareness is the foundation for personal growth and development. It is the ability to understand oneself, one's thoughts, emotions, and behaviors. Developing self-awareness is a lifelong process, but it is worth the effort. By becoming more self-aware, we can make better decisions, improve our relationships, manage stress and anxiety, and develop resilience and adaptability. It is the key to unlocking our true potential and living a fulfilling life.

03: The Benefits of Self-Awareness: Why It Matters in the Modern World

Introduction

Self-awareness is a powerful tool that can help you lead a more fulfilling life in the modern world. It allows you to understand your thoughts, emotions, and behaviors, and how they affect your life and relationships. In this chapter, we will explore the benefits of self-awareness and how it can transform your life.

The Benefits of Self-Awareness

Improved Emotional Intelligence

Emotional intelligence is the ability to understand and manage your emotions and the emotions of others. Self-awareness is a critical component of emotional intelligence. When you are self-aware, you can recognize your emotions and how they influence your thoughts and actions. This knowledge helps you regulate your emotions, make better decisions, and communicate more effectively.

03: THE BENEFITS OF SELF-AWARENESS: WHY IT MATTERS IN THE MODERN WORLD

Greater Self-Acceptance

Self-awareness helps you recognize your strengths and weaknesses without judgment. This knowledge allows you to accept yourself for who you are, flaws and all. When you accept yourself, you can stop trying to be someone you're not and start focusing on your unique talents and abilities. This self-acceptance leads to increased self-esteem and confidence.

Enhanced Self-Control

Self-awareness helps you understand your triggers and how to manage them. When you know what sets you off, you can prepare yourself to respond differently. For example, if you know that you get angry when someone interrupts you, you can practice responding calmly and assertively when it happens. This self-control allows you to manage your impulses and make better choices.

Improved Decision Making

When you are self-aware, you can make decisions that align with your values and goals. You can recognize when you are making decisions based on fear or other emotions and choose a different course of action. This ability to make conscious, deliberate choices leads to better outcomes in all areas of life.

Better Communication

Self-awareness helps you communicate more effectively with others. When you understand your emotions and how they influence your communication style, you can adjust your approach to better meet the needs of the person you are talking to. For example, if you tend to be blunt when you are frustrated, you can learn to express your frustration in a more constructive way that doesn't hurt the other person's feelings.

Deeper Relationships

Self-awareness allows you to understand how you contribute to your relationships. When you recognize your patterns of behavior and how they affect others, you can make changes that strengthen your connections. For example, if you tend to be critical of your partner, you can learn to express your concerns in a more constructive way that doesn't damage your relationship.

Increased Empathy

Empathy is the ability to understand and feel the emotions of others. When you are self-aware, you can recognize your own emotions and how they relate to the emotions of others. This knowledge allows you to empathize with others on a deeper level and respond to their needs in a more meaningful way.

Greater Resilience

Self-awareness helps you bounce back from setbacks and challenges. When you understand your own emotions and how they influence your responses to stress, you can develop coping strategies that work for you. This resilience allows you to face challenges with confidence and move forward with your goals.

Improved Creativity

Self-awareness allows you to tap into your creative potential. When you understand your thoughts, feelings, and behaviors, you can use that knowledge to generate new ideas and approaches. This creativity can lead to innovation in all areas of life, from work to relationships to hobbies.

Greater Personal Growth

Self-awareness is the foundation of personal growth. When you are aware of your thoughts, emotions, and behaviors, you can identify areas for improvement and take action to make positive changes. This growth leads to a more fulfilling life and a greater sense of purpose.

Conclusion

Self-awareness is a powerful tool that can transform your life in countless ways. From improving your emotional intelligence to enhancing your creativity, the benefits of self-awareness are numerous and far-reaching. By cultivating self-awareness, you can develop a greater understanding of yourself and the world around you, and make conscious, deliberate choices that lead to a more fulfilling life.

However, developing self-awareness is not always easy. It requires introspection, reflection, and a willingness to be honest with yourself about your thoughts, feelings, and behaviors. It also requires a commitment to ongoing personal growth and a willingness to embrace change.

Fortunately, there are many resources available to help you develop self-awareness, from mindfulness practices to therapy to self-help books like this one. The key is to find the tools and techniques that work best for you and to commit to using them consistently over time.

In the next chapter, we will explore some of the obstacles that can prevent us from developing self-awareness, as well as strategies for overcoming them. We will also discuss some of the common myths and misconceptions about self-awareness, and how to navigate them on your path to personal growth and transformation.

04: Developing Self-Awareness: A Step-by-Step Guide

Introduction:

Self-awareness is a crucial aspect of personal growth and development. It is the ability to objectively observe and understand your thoughts, feelings, and behaviors. Self-awareness allows you to identify your strengths and weaknesses, recognize your patterns, and make informed decisions that align with your values and goals. This chapter will provide you with a step-by-step guide to developing self-awareness.

Step 1: Practice Mindfulness

The first step in developing self-awareness is to practice mindfulness. Mindfulness is the practice of paying attention to the present moment without judgment. By becoming more aware of your thoughts and feelings, you can better understand yourself and your reactions to different situations. One way to practice mindfulness is to meditate. Meditation is a technique that involves focusing your attention on a particular object, such as your breath, and observing your thoughts without judgment. Meditation can help you develop a more focused and clear mind, which is essential for developing self-awareness.

Step 2: Keep a Journal

Keeping a journal is another way to develop self-awareness. Journaling allows you to reflect on your experiences, thoughts, and emotions. By writing down your thoughts and feelings, you can gain a deeper understanding of yourself and your patterns. You can also use your journal to set goals and track your progress. Journaling can be a helpful tool for identifying areas where you need to improve and developing strategies for growth.

Step 3: Seek Feedback

Seeking feedback from others is a critical step in developing self-awareness. Feedback from others can provide you with valuable insights into your strengths and weaknesses. It can also help you identify blind spots that you may not be aware of. When seeking feedback, it is essential to be open-minded and receptive to criticism. Remember that feedback is not a personal attack, but rather an opportunity for growth.

Step 4: Identify Your Values

Identifying your values is another essential step in developing self-awareness. Your values are the principles that guide your behavior and decision-making. They are the things that are most important to you. By identifying your values, you can gain a deeper understanding of yourself and your motivations. You can also use your values as a guide for making decisions that align with your goals and aspirations.

Step 5: Identify Your Triggers

Identifying your triggers is another critical step in developing self-awareness. Triggers are the things that cause you to react emotionally. They can be situations, people, or things that remind you of past experiences. By identifying your triggers, you can learn to manage your emotional reactions and respond in a more constructive way. You can also use your triggers as a guide for understanding your patterns and behaviors.

Step 6: Practice Self-Reflection

Practicing self-reflection is another important step in developing self-awareness. Self-reflection is the process of examining your thoughts, feelings, and behaviors. It can help you identify patterns and make connections between your experiences. By reflecting on your experiences, you can gain a deeper understanding of yourself and your motivations. You can also use self-reflection to identify areas where you need to improve and develop strategies for growth.

Step 7: Identify Your Strengths and Weaknesses

Identifying your strengths and weaknesses is another crucial step in developing self-awareness. Your strengths are the things that you excel at, while your weaknesses are the areas where you need improvement. By identifying your strengths and weaknesses, you can develop strategies to maximize your strengths and overcome your weaknesses. You can also use this information to set goals that align with your strengths and work on improving your weaknesses.

Step 8: Embrace Your Emotions

Finally, it is essential to embrace your emotions in the process of developing self-awareness. Emotions are a natural part of being human. By embracing your emotions, you can

better understand your internal experiences and use them

as a guide for your decisions and actions. When you experience emotions, try to label them and understand what triggers them. This way, you can identify patterns and gain insight into how you respond to certain situations.

It is also important to acknowledge that some emotions may be uncomfortable or difficult to process. However, suppressing or denying these emotions can lead to negative consequences, such as increased stress and anxiety. Instead, try to accept and process your emotions in a healthy and constructive way, such as by talking to a trusted friend or therapist.

Conclusion:

Developing self-awareness is an ongoing process that requires patience, dedication, and practice. By following these steps, you can gain a deeper understanding of yourself and your motivations, which can help you make informed decisions and live a more fulfilling life. Remember to be kind and patient with yourself throughout this journey, as developing self-awareness is not an easy or quick process. With persistence and effort, you can unlock your true potential and live a life that aligns with your values and aspirations.

05: Mindfulness and Self-Awareness: The Connection and How to Practice It

Introduction

The concept of self-awareness has been around for centuries, and it's an essential component of personal growth and development. Self-awareness is the ability to understand one's own thoughts, feelings, and behaviors. It's an introspective process that requires you to take a step back and examine yourself objectively. One way to develop self-awareness is through mindfulness practice. In this chapter, we'll explore the connection between mindfulness and self-awareness and how to practice mindfulness to increase our self-awareness.

What is Mindfulness?

Mindfulness is the practice of being present and fully engaged in the current moment. It's the ability to observe your thoughts, feelings, and sensations without judgment. Mindfulness involves paying attention to your breath, your body, and your surroundings. It's a state of active awareness that allows you to be fully present in the moment.

05: MINDFULNESS AND SELF-AWARENESS: THE CONNECTION AND HOW TO PRACTICE IT

There are many benefits to practicing mindfulness, including reducing stress and anxiety, improving focus and concentration, and increasing self-awareness. Mindfulness has been shown to improve mental health and well-being and can be used as a tool for personal growth and transformation.

The Connection Between Mindfulness and Self-Awareness

Mindfulness and self-awareness are interconnected. Mindfulness allows us to observe our thoughts and feelings without judgment, which is essential for developing self-awareness. When we practice mindfulness, we become more aware of our thoughts, feelings, and behaviors. We learn to observe ourselves objectively and identify patterns and habits that may be holding us back.

Mindfulness also helps us to develop a deeper understanding of ourselves. By observing our thoughts and feelings, we can identify our values, beliefs, and motivations. This self-awareness allows us to make better decisions and take actions that align with our goals and values.

How to Practice Mindfulness for Self-Awareness

05: MINDFULNESS AND SELF-AWARENESS: THE CONNECTION AND HOW TO PRACTICE IT

There are many ways to practice mindfulness, and the best approach will vary depending on your preferences and lifestyle. Here are some ways to practice mindfulness to increase your self-awareness:

Mindful Breathing: One of the most accessible ways to practice mindfulness is through mindful breathing. Find a quiet place to sit comfortably and focus your attention on your breath. Notice the sensation of the air moving in and out of your body. If your mind wanders, gently bring your attention back to your breath.

Body Scan: Another way to practice mindfulness is through a body scan. Lie down on your back and bring your attention to each part of your body, starting with your toes and moving up to the top of your head. Notice any sensations or discomfort in each area without judgment.

Mindful Eating: Mindful eating is an excellent way to practice mindfulness while nourishing your body. Take the time to savor each bite of your food, noticing the flavor, texture, and aroma. Pay attention to your body's signals of hunger and fullness.

05: MINDFULNESS AND SELF-AWARENESS: THE CONNECTION AND HOW TO PRACTICE IT

Mindful Walking: Walking can be a mindful practice if you approach it with intention. Focus on the sensation of your feet touching the ground and the movement of your body as you walk. Notice the sights, sounds, and smells around you.

Mindful Meditation: Mindful meditation involves sitting quietly and bringing your attention to the present moment. You can focus on your breath, a sound, or a visual object. When your mind wanders, gently bring your attention back to your chosen focus.

Conclusion

Mindfulness is a powerful tool for developing self-awareness. By practicing mindfulness, we learn to observe ourselves without judgment and develop a deeper understanding of our thoughts, feelings, and behaviors. Mindfulness can be practiced in many ways, from mindful breathing to mindful eating to mindful meditation. Incorporating mindfulness into your daily routine can help you increase your self-awareness, reduce stress and anxiety, and improve your overall well-being.

06: The Role of Emotions in Self-Awareness: How to Manage and Use Them

Introduction

Emotions are an integral part of our daily lives, and they play a crucial role in our self-awareness. We experience a range of emotions, from joy and excitement to fear and anger, and everything in between. It is essential to understand the role of emotions in self-awareness, how to manage them, and how to use them to our advantage. This chapter will explore the significance of emotions in self-awareness and provide practical tips for managing and using them.

The Importance of Emotions in Self-Awareness

Emotions are the primary indicator of our well-being and reflect our internal state. They are an essential aspect of our self-awareness, and understanding them can help us navigate our lives more effectively. Emotions can influence our thoughts, behaviors, and actions, and when we are aware of them, we can respond more intentionally and purposefully.

Emotions also provide us with valuable information about

ourselves and the world around us. For instance, fear can signal danger, and sadness can indicate a loss. When we pay attention to our emotions, we can identify the underlying causes and take appropriate action. Moreover, emotions can help us connect with others and foster empathy and understanding.

However, emotions can also be overwhelming and challenging to manage, especially when we experience intense or conflicting emotions. It is essential to learn how to manage our emotions effectively to avoid becoming overwhelmed and making impulsive decisions.

How to Manage Emotions

Emotions are not something we can control, but we can manage how we respond to them. Here are some practical tips for managing emotions:

– Identify the emotion: The first step in managing emotions is to identify what we are feeling. Naming the emotion can help us understand it better and reduce its intensity.

– Accept the emotion: It is essential to accept the emotion

without judgment. Suppressing or ignoring emotions can make them more intense and challenging to manage.

– Explore the trigger: Understanding the cause of the emotion can help us manage it better. Identifying triggers can also help us avoid or prepare for situations that may cause intense emotions.

– Engage in self-care: Practicing self-care can help regulate emotions. Activities like exercise, meditation, or talking to a trusted friend or therapist can help reduce stress and promote emotional well-being.

– Practice mindfulness: Mindfulness involves being present in the moment without judgment. It can help us observe our emotions without becoming overwhelmed by them.

– Develop healthy coping strategies: Developing healthy coping strategies like journaling, drawing, or deep breathing can help us manage intense emotions.

How to Use Emotions

Emotions can also be used to our advantage when we learn how to harness their power. Here are some practical tips for

06: THE ROLE OF EMOTIONS IN SELF-AWARENESS: HOW TO MANAGE AND USE THEM

using emotions:

– Use emotions as motivation: Emotions like excitement or enthusiasm can motivate us to pursue our goals and achieve our aspirations.

– Harness the power of positive emotions: Positive emotions like joy and gratitude can increase resilience, well-being, and positive relationships.

– Use emotions to connect with others: Emotions can help us empathize and connect with others. Sharing our emotions with others can foster deep and meaningful connections.

– Use emotions to improve decision-making: Emotions can provide valuable information that can improve decision-making. For example, feelings of unease can indicate a potential problem, and positive emotions can indicate a good opportunity.

Conclusion

Emotions are an integral part of our self-awareness, and understanding how to manage and use them can help us navigate our lives more effectively. Emotions can provide valuable information about ourselves and the world around us, but they can also be overwhelming and challenging to manage. By practicing emotional management and harnessing the power of emotions, we can improve our well-being, relationships, and decision-making. It is essential to develop a healthy relationship with our emotions and recognize that they are a natural part of being human. By learning how to manage and use them effectively, we can unlock our true potential and live a fulfilling life in the modern world.

Self-awareness is a journey that requires continuous effort and practice. Emotions are just one aspect of self-awareness, but they play a critical role in shaping our experiences and perceptions of the world around us. By paying attention to our emotions and developing healthy emotional management strategies, we can cultivate a more robust sense of self-awareness and live a more fulfilling life.

Remember that emotions are not something to be ashamed of or to ignore. They are a natural part of our internal experience and can provide valuable information about ourselves and the world around us. By embracing our emotions and learning how to manage them effectively, we can develop a deeper understanding of ourselves and others, improve our relationships, and achieve our goals.

In conclusion, self-awareness is a crucial component of personal growth and transformation, and emotions are an essential aspect of self-awareness. By learning how to manage and use our emotions effectively, we can cultivate a more robust sense of self-awareness, improve our well-being and relationships, and live a more fulfilling life. The journey to self-awareness may not be easy, but it is worth the effort, and it starts with learning how to manage our emotions.

07: Self-Reflection: Techniques to Gain Insight and Improve Self-Awareness

Introduction

Self-awareness is the foundation of personal growth and transformation. Without self-awareness, it is impossible to identify our strengths, weaknesses, values, and beliefs, and understand how they shape our thoughts, emotions, and behavior. In today's fast-paced and complex world, self-awareness is more important than ever. It helps us navigate the challenges and opportunities of modern life, make better decisions, build stronger relationships, and achieve our goals.

Self-reflection is one of the most powerful techniques for gaining insight and improving self-awareness. It involves examining our thoughts, emotions, and behavior, and exploring their underlying causes and consequences. Through self-reflection, we can identify our patterns, biases, and blind spots, and develop a deeper understanding of ourselves and our relationship with the world.

In this chapter, we will explore various techniques for self-reflection and how they can be used to enhance self-awareness and personal growth.

Journaling

Journaling is one of the most popular and effective techniques for self-reflection. It involves writing down our thoughts, emotions, and experiences in a journal or notebook. Journaling can help us identify patterns, themes, and insights that we might not otherwise notice. It also provides a space for self-expression, self-compassion, and self-reflection.

To start journaling, set aside a regular time each day or week to write. Find a quiet and comfortable place where you can focus on your thoughts and feelings without distractions. Begin by writing whatever comes to mind, without worrying about grammar, spelling, or punctuation. Write as if you were talking to yourself or a trusted friend, and be honest and non-judgmental.

Some prompts for journaling might include:

– What am I feeling right now, and why?

07: SELF-REFLECTION: TECHNIQUES TO GAIN IN-SIGHT AND IMPROVE SELF-AWARENESS

– What are my goals and aspirations, and how am I working towards them?

– What are my fears and doubts, and how can I overcome them?

– What are my values and beliefs, and how do they guide my decisions?

– What are some of my patterns and habits, and how do they affect my life?

Reflective Questioning

Reflective questioning is a technique that involves asking ourselves open-ended questions to explore our thoughts, emotions, and behavior. Reflective questioning can help us uncover underlying assumptions, biases, and motivations, and gain a deeper understanding of ourselves and our relationship with the world.

To use reflective questioning, start by asking yourself a question about a particular experience or situation. Then, allow yourself time to reflect on the question and your response. Be open and curious, and explore your thoughts and feelings without judgment or criticism.

Some examples of reflective questions might include:

– What was my role in this situation, and how did I contribute to the outcome?

– What are some of the assumptions or beliefs that underlie
my behavior, and are they accurate or helpful?

– What are some of the emotions I am experiencing right
now, and what are their underlying causes?

– What are some of the lessons I can learn from this experience, and how can I apply them in the future?

Meditation

Meditation is a practice that involves focusing our attention
on a particular object or sensation, such as the breath or a
mantra. Meditation can help us cultivate mindfulness,
which is the ability to be present and aware of our thoughts,
emotions, and sensations without judgment or distraction.

To meditate, find a quiet and comfortable place where you

can sit or lie down without distractions. Set a timer for a desired amount of time, and close your eyes or focus on a particular object. Begin by focusing on your breath, and notice the sensations of inhaling and exhaling. If your mind wanders, gently bring it back to the breath without judgment or criticism.

Meditation can be a powerful tool for self-reflection, as it helps us observe our thoughts and emotions without getting caught up in them. As we meditate regularly, we can develop a greater awareness of our internal state, and begin to notice patterns and tendencies that might be affecting our well-being and behavior.

Body Scan

The body scan is a technique that involves systematically bringing our attention to different parts of our body and noticing the sensations we experience. The body scan can help us connect with our physical selves and become more aware of any tension, discomfort, or other sensations we might be experiencing.

To do a body scan, find a quiet and comfortable place where

you can lie down without distractions. Begin by focusing on your breath, and then gradually move your attention to different parts of your body, starting with your toes and moving upwards towards your head.

As you focus on each part of your body, notice any sensations you experience, such as tension, warmth, or tingling. Try to observe these sensations without judgment or interpretation, simply noticing what is there. If you notice any tension or discomfort, try to relax that part of your body as much as possible.

The body scan can be a helpful tool for self-reflection, as it allows us to become more aware of the physical sensations associated with our emotions and thoughts. By noticing these sensations, we can gain insight into our internal state and begin to address any underlying issues.

Creative Expression

Creative expression is a technique that involves using art, music, writing, or other forms of self-expression to explore our thoughts, emotions, and experiences. Creative expression can help us tap into our unconscious mind and bring to

light aspects of ourselves that might be difficult to express
through words alone.

To use creative expression for self-reflection, choose a form
of expression that resonates with you, such as drawing,
painting, playing music, or writing poetry. Set aside a regular time to engage in this activity, and allow yourself to express whatever comes to mind without judgment or censor-
ship.

As you engage in creative expression, pay attention to the
thoughts, emotions, and sensations that arise. Notice how
your creative output reflects your internal state, and look
for patterns or themes that emerge. Consider sharing your
creations with others, either through social media, art
shows, or other venues, as a way to connect with others and
gain feedback.

Conclusion

Self-reflection is a powerful tool for gaining insight and improving self-awareness. By using techniques such as journaling, reflective questioning, meditation, body scanning,
and creative expression, we can explore our thoughts, emo-

tions, and behavior in a non-judgmental and compassionate way. Through self-reflection, we can gain a deeper understanding of ourselves and our relationship with the world, and cultivate the self-awareness necessary to live a fulfilling life in the modern world.

08: Self-Observation: How to Observe Your Thoughts, Feelings, and Behaviors

Introduction

Self-awareness is an essential component of personal growth and transformation. It is the ability to understand your thoughts, emotions, and behaviors and how they influence your life. In this chapter, we will explore self-observation, a powerful technique that can help you develop self-awareness. We will discuss what self-observation is, why it is important, and how to practice it.

What is Self-Observation?

Self-observation is the practice of observing your thoughts, emotions, and behaviors without judgment. It is a tool that can help you become more aware of your inner world and how it affects your outer world. Self-observation is not about analyzing or interpreting your experiences but rather about observing them objectively.

Why is Self-Observation Important?

08: SELF-OBSERVATION: HOW TO OBSERVE YOUR THOUGHTS, FEELINGS, AND BEHAVIORS

Self-observation is important for several reasons. First, it can help you identify patterns in your thoughts, emotions, and behaviors. By observing yourself, you can begin to notice recurring themes and tendencies that may be hindering your personal growth. Second, self-observation can help you become more self-aware. When you are aware of your thoughts, emotions, and behaviors, you can make conscious choices about how to respond to them. Finally, self-observation can help you cultivate mindfulness, which can lead to greater inner peace and a sense of well-being.

How to Practice Self-Observation

Practicing self-observation requires a willingness to be honest with yourself and a commitment to self-awareness. Here are some steps you can take to begin practicing self-observation:

Set aside time for self-observation. Find a quiet place where you can be alone with your thoughts. You may want to set aside a specific time each day for self-observation.

Focus your attention on your thoughts, emotions, and behaviors. Pay attention to what you are thinking, feeling, and doing. Try to observe yourself objectively, without judgment.

Write down your observations. Keeping a journal can be a helpful tool for self-observation. Write down what you observe about yourself, including any recurring patterns or themes.

Be open to feedback. Ask trusted friends or family members for feedback on your behavior. Their observations may help you become more aware of your tendencies and patterns.

Practice mindfulness. Mindfulness is the practice of being fully present in the moment. When you are mindful, you are more aware of your thoughts, emotions, and behaviors. Practicing mindfulness can help you become more self-aware and improve your ability to observe yourself.

Conclusion

Self-observation is a powerful tool for developing self-awareness. By observing your thoughts, emotions, and behaviors, you can identify patterns and tendencies that may be holding you back. Practicing self-observation requires a willingness to be honest with yourself and a commitment to self-awareness. By making self-observation a regular part of your life, you can develop greater self-awareness and live a more fulfilling life.

09: Self-Talk: The Impact of Our Internal Dialogue on Self-Awareness

Introduction

Self-talk, also known as our internal dialogue, is the voice in our heads that narrates our thoughts, feelings, and experiences. It is a constant companion that shapes our perceptions of the world, ourselves, and others. Whether we are aware of it or not, our self-talk has a profound impact on our emotions, behaviors, and overall well-being. In this chapter, we will explore the importance of self-talk in developing self-awareness and living a fulfilling life.

Understanding Self-Talk

Self-talk can be positive or negative, and it is often influenced by our beliefs, experiences, and emotions. Positive self-talk involves using affirmations and optimistic language to encourage and motivate ourselves. Negative self-talk, on the other hand, is characterized by self-criticism, self-doubt, and pessimism. It can lead to feelings of anxiety, depression, and low self-esteem.

09: SELF-TALK: THE IMPACT OF OUR INTERNAL DIALOGUE ON SELF-AWARENESS

Self-talk is not just limited to our conscious thoughts. It can also be automatic and habitual, based on deep-rooted beliefs and assumptions. For example, if we have a belief that we are not good enough, our self-talk may reflect that belief by telling us that we are not capable of achieving our goals or that we do not deserve success.

The Impact of Self-Talk on Self-Awareness

Self-awareness is the ability to recognize and understand our emotions, thoughts, and behaviors. It is a critical component of personal growth and development. Self-talk plays a significant role in developing self-awareness because it influences how we interpret and respond to our experiences.

When we practice positive self-talk, we are more likely to have a growth mindset and be open to learning from our mistakes. This allows us to develop a deeper understanding of ourselves and our motivations. Positive self-talk can also help us to regulate our emotions and cope with stress more effectively.

Conversely, negative self-talk can limit our self-awareness by reinforcing limiting beliefs and negative self-perceptions.

It can lead to a fixed mindset, where we believe that our abilities and qualities are fixed and unchangeable. This can prevent us from taking risks, trying new things, and reaching our full potential.

Practicing Positive Self-Talk

Practicing positive self-talk is a powerful tool for developing self-awareness and building resilience. Here are some tips for cultivating positive self-talk:

Identify Negative Self-Talk

The first step in changing our self-talk is to become aware of it. Pay attention to the thoughts and language you use when you talk to yourself. If you notice any negative self-talk, challenge it by asking yourself if it is based on fact or if it is just a negative belief.

Reframe Negative Thoughts

Once you have identified negative self-talk, reframe it into positive statements. For example, instead of saying, "I can't do this," say, "I am capable of learning and growing." This will help to shift your mindset from a fixed mindset to a growth mindset.

Use Affirmations

Affirmations are positive statements that you repeat to yourself to reinforce positive beliefs and attitudes. Choose affirmations that are meaningful to you and repeat them regularly. For example, "I am worthy of love and respect," or "I am capable of achieving my goals."

Practice Gratitude

Practicing gratitude can help to shift your focus from what you don't have to what you do have. Take time each day to reflect on the things you are grateful for, and focus on the positive aspects of your life.

Surround Yourself with Positive Influences

Surrounding yourself with positive influences, such as supportive friends and family, can help to reinforce positive self-talk and beliefs. Seek out people who inspire and motivate you, and limit your exposure to negative influences.

Conclusion

09: SELF-TALK: THE IMPACT OF OUR INTERNAL DIA-LOGUE ON SELF-AWARENESS

In conclusion, self-talk is a powerful tool that can either support or hinder our personal growth and self-awareness. By becoming aware of our internal dialogue and learning to reframe negative thoughts into positive ones, we can develop a growth mindset and build resilience in the face of challenges.

Practicing positive self-talk requires time and effort, but the rewards are well worth it. With a more positive and optimistic outlook, we can improve our relationships, achieve our goals, and live a more fulfilling life.

Remember, the words we say to ourselves have a profound impact on our emotions, behaviors, and overall well-being. By cultivating positive self-talk, we can unlock our true potential and become the best version of ourselves.

10: Self-Acceptance: Embracing Your Strengths and Weaknesses for Personal Growth

Introduction

Self-acceptance is one of the most important aspects of self-awareness. It is the act of embracing who we are, both our strengths and our weaknesses. When we learn to accept ourselves, we become more resilient, confident, and authentic. It is a powerful tool that helps us in our personal growth journey.

In this chapter, we will explore the concept of self-acceptance and how it can help us to become the best version of ourselves. We will delve into the benefits of self-acceptance, the barriers that prevent us from accepting ourselves, and practical strategies to cultivate self-acceptance.

The Importance of Self-Acceptance

Self-acceptance is crucial to our well-being and personal growth. It enables us to embrace our true selves, rather than trying to fit into a mold created by others. When we accept ourselves, we become more confident in our abilities and less critical of our flaws. We are more able to focus on our strengths and use them to achieve our goals.

Furthermore, self-acceptance is linked to better mental health outcomes. It reduces stress, anxiety, and depression, and increases our resilience in the face of challenges. Studies have shown that individuals who have a higher level of self-acceptance tend to have better relationships, higher self-esteem, and greater life satisfaction.

Barriers to Self-Acceptance

Despite the importance of self-acceptance, many of us struggle with accepting ourselves. This may be due to societal expectations, negative experiences in our past, or our own inner critic. Here are some common barriers to self-acceptance:

Comparing ourselves to others: When we compare ourselves to others, we set unrealistic expectations for ourselves. This can lead to feelings of inadequacy and a lack of self-acceptance.

Perfectionism: When we strive for perfection, we set

ourselves up for failure. No one is perfect, and expecting ourselves to be perfect can prevent us from accepting ourselves.

Negative self-talk: Our inner critic can be harsh, and often prevents us from accepting ourselves. We may focus on our flaws and mistakes, rather than our strengths and achievements.

Past experiences: Negative experiences in our past can also prevent us from accepting ourselves. This may be due to past traumas, rejection, or criticism.

Strategies for Cultivating Self-Acceptance

Despite the barriers to self-acceptance, it is possible to cultivate this powerful tool. Here are some strategies for cultivating self-acceptance:

Practice self-compassion: Treat yourself with the same kindness and understanding that you would offer a good friend. Be gentle with yourself when you make mistakes, and focus on your strengths.

10: SELF-ACCEPTANCE: EMBRACING YOUR STRENGTHS AND WEAKNESSES FOR PERSONAL GROWTH

Focus on the present moment: Let go of the past and future, and focus on the present moment. This can help you to become more aware of your thoughts and emotions, and to accept them without judgment.

Challenge negative self-talk: When your inner critic starts to speak, challenge it with positive affirmations. Remind yourself of your strengths and accomplishments, and focus on your progress rather than your mistakes.

Embrace your imperfections: Embrace your imperfections and recognize that they make you unique. Learn to love yourself for who you are, flaws and all.

Surround yourself with positivity: Surround yourself with positive people who accept and support you. This can help you to cultivate a positive self-image and to become more accepting of yourself.

Conclusion

Self-acceptance is a powerful tool that can help us to become the best version of ourselves. It enables us to embrace our strengths and weaknesses, and to become more authen-

10: SELF-ACCEPTANCE: EMBRACING YOUR STRENGTHS AND WEAKNESSES FOR PERSONAL GROWTH

tic and confident. Despite the barriers to self-acceptance, it is possible to cultivate this important trait through self-compassion, mindfulness, challenging negative self-talk, embracing imperfections, and surrounding ourselves with positivity.

Self-acceptance is not a one-time event; it is a continuous process that requires effort and practice. It is important to remember that self-acceptance does not mean that we are perfect or that we do not have room for improvement. It means that we are aware of our strengths and weaknesses and that we accept ourselves for who we are, flaws and all.

As we continue to practice self-acceptance, we may find that we become more resilient in the face of challenges. We may become more confident in our abilities and more willing to take risks. We may also find that we become more compassionate towards ourselves and others.

In conclusion, self-acceptance is a vital aspect of self-awareness and personal growth. It enables us to embrace our true selves and to become more authentic, resilient, and confident. By practicing self-compassion, mindfulness, and positive self-talk, we can cultivate self-acceptance and live a more fulfilling life.

11: Self-Compassion: Why It Matters and How to Practice It

Self-compassion is the practice of treating ourselves with the same kindness, care, and understanding that we would offer to a good friend. It involves being aware of our own suffering and responding with warmth and concern rather than self-criticism or self-judgment. Self-compassion is a crucial component of self-awareness, as it allows us to acknowledge and accept our flaws and imperfections while still striving for personal growth and transformation. In this chapter, we will explore why self-compassion matters and provide practical tips and techniques for cultivating this important skill in our daily lives.

Why Self-Compassion Matters

Self-compassion is essential for our emotional well-being and mental health. When we are kind to ourselves, we are less likely to experience stress, anxiety, depression, and other negative emotions. We are also more resilient in the face of adversity, as self-compassion provides us with a sense of inner strength and stability.

In contrast, when we are self-critical or self-judging, we undermine our self-esteem and confidence. We may become trapped in a cycle of negative self-talk, constantly berating ourselves for our mistakes or perceived shortcomings. This can lead to feelings of shame, guilt, and worthlessness, which can have a significant impact on our overall quality of life.

Self-compassion is also important for our relationships with others. When we are kind and compassionate to ourselves, we are better able to offer the same to others. We are more empathetic and understanding, and we are less likely to project our own insecurities and fears onto others. This allows us to build stronger, more authentic connections with the people around us.

How to Practice Self-Compassion

Practicing self-compassion involves several key elements, including self-kindness, mindfulness, and common humanity. Here are some tips and techniques for cultivating self-compassion in your daily life:

Practice Self-Kindness

11: SELF-COMPASSION: WHY IT MATTERS AND HOW TO PRACTICE IT

The first step in practicing self-compassion is to be kind and gentle with yourself. When you make a mistake or experience a setback, try to offer yourself the same compassion and support that you would offer to a good friend. Instead of beating yourself up or engaging in negative self-talk, remind yourself that everyone makes mistakes and that you are doing the best you can.

Practice Mindfulness

Mindfulness is the practice of being fully present and aware of the present moment, without judgment or distraction. By practicing mindfulness, we can become more aware of our thoughts, emotions, and physical sensations, and we can learn to respond to them with compassion and understanding.

To practice mindfulness, try to set aside some time each day to sit quietly and focus on your breath. As thoughts and emotions arise, simply observe them without judgment, and then return your attention to your breath. With practice, you can learn to become more present and aware in your daily life, and you can respond to your thoughts and emotions with greater self-compassion.

11: SELF-COMPASSION: WHY IT MATTERS AND HOW TO PRACTICE IT

Cultivate Common Humanity

Finally, it is important to remember that we are all human and that we all experience suffering and challenges in our lives. By cultivating a sense of common humanity, we can recognize that our struggles are not unique and that we are not alone in our pain.

To cultivate common humanity, try to connect with others who share your experiences or challenges. Join a support group, reach out to a friend, or seek the guidance of a therapist or counselor. By sharing your struggles with others, you can gain perspective and support, and you can develop a greater sense of compassion and empathy for yourself and others.

In conclusion, self-compassion is a crucial skill for personal growth and transformation. By treating ourselves with kindness, mindfulness, and common humanity, we can cultivate greater emotional well-being, mental health, and authentic connections with others. However, like any skill, self-compassion requires practice and dedication. Here are some additional tips and techniques for cultivating self-compassion in your daily life:

11: SELF-COMPASSION: WHY IT MATTERS AND HOW TO PRACTICE IT

Practice Gratitude

Gratitude is the practice of acknowledging and appreciating the good things in our lives, both big and small. By cultivating a sense of gratitude, we can shift our focus away from our problems and toward the positive aspects of our lives.

To practice gratitude, try to set aside some time each day to reflect on the things you are thankful for. Write them down in a journal or simply take a few moments to express gratitude silently to yourself. By focusing on the good in your life, you can cultivate a sense of contentment and joy, which can in turn help you to be more compassionate toward yourself and others.

Challenge Negative Self-Talk

Negative self-talk is the inner dialogue we have with ourselves, often characterized by self-criticism, self-doubt, and self-blame. This type of thinking can be detrimental to our emotional well-being and can prevent us from reaching our full potential.

To challenge negative self-talk, try to become more aware of your inner dialogue. When you notice negative thoughts creeping in, try to reframe them in a more positive or compassionate light. For example, if you find yourself thinking, "I'm so stupid," try to reframe it as, "I made a mistake, but that doesn't define my worth as a person." By challenging negative self-talk, you can cultivate a more compassionate and positive inner voice.

Practice Self-Care

Self-care is the practice of taking care of yourself, both physically and emotionally. This can involve a range of activities, from getting enough sleep and exercise to engaging in hobbies and self-reflection.

To practice self-care, try to set aside some time each day to do something that nourishes your body or soul. This could be as simple as taking a walk in nature or listening to your favorite music. By prioritizing self-care, you can cultivate a greater sense of well-being and resilience, which can in turn help you to be more compassionate toward yourself and others.

In conclusion, self-compassion is a powerful tool for personal growth and transformation. By cultivating self-kindness, mindfulness, and common humanity, and by practicing gratitude, challenging negative self-talk, and prioritizing self-care, you can develop a more compassionate and authentic relationship with yourself and others. Remember, self-compassion is a journey, not a destination, and it requires ongoing practice and dedication. But by making self-compassion a priority in your life, you can unlock your true potential and live a more fulfilling and meaningful life in the modern world.

12: Self-Confidence: Building a Strong Sense of Self-Worth

Self-confidence is the foundation upon which we build our lives. It is a fundamental component of our well-being and a critical factor in achieving success and happiness. A strong sense of self-worth is essential to our ability to navigate life's challenges, pursue our goals, and realize our dreams. Without self-confidence, we may find ourselves stuck in a cycle of self-doubt and self-sabotage, unable to achieve the success and happiness we desire. In this chapter, we will explore the nature of self-confidence, its importance in our lives, and strategies for building a strong sense of self-worth.

What is self-confidence?

Self-confidence is the belief in one's abilities, qualities, and judgment. It is the sense of trust in oneself that allows us to take risks, make decisions, and pursue our goals. Self-confidence is not a static trait; it is something that can be developed and cultivated over time. While some individuals may be naturally more self-confident than others, everyone has the capacity to build their sense of self-worth.

12: SELF-CONFIDENCE: BUILDING A STRONG SENSE OF SELF-WORTH

Why is self-confidence important?

Self-confidence is critical to our ability to achieve our goals and fulfill our potential. When we believe in ourselves, we are more likely to take action and pursue our dreams. We are less likely to be deterred by setbacks or failures and more likely to bounce back from adversity. Self-confidence also helps us to build stronger relationships, communicate more effectively, and assert ourselves in social and professional situations. A strong sense of self-worth can improve our mental health and well-being, reduce stress and anxiety, and enhance our overall quality of life.

Strategies for building self-confidence

Practice self-compassion

Self-compassion is the practice of treating oneself with kindness, understanding, and forgiveness. It involves acknowledging our flaws and imperfections without judgment or self-criticism. By cultivating self-compassion, we can build a more positive and nurturing relationship with ourselves, which can improve our sense of self-worth and self-confidence.

12: SELF-CONFIDENCE: BUILDING A STRONG SENSE OF SELF-WORTH

Challenge negative self-talk

Negative self-talk is the inner dialogue that undermines our confidence and self-worth. It can take the form of self-doubt, self-criticism, or self-sabotage. By challenging negative self-talk and replacing it with positive affirmations, we can build a more supportive and empowering inner dialogue.

Set achievable goals

Setting achievable goals and working towards them can improve our sense of self-efficacy and confidence. By breaking down larger goals into smaller, more manageable steps, we can build momentum and progress towards our desired outcome. Celebrating our achievements along the way can also reinforce our sense of self-worth and confidence.

Practice self-care

Self-care involves taking care of our physical, emotional, and mental well-being. By prioritizing self-care, we can reduce stress and anxiety, improve our mood and energy levels, and enhance our overall sense of well-being. This, in

turn, can improve our sense of self-worth and self-confidence.

Seek support

Building self-confidence can be challenging, and it is important to seek support when needed. This can involve
reaching out to friends and family for encouragement or
seeking the help of a therapist or coach to work through issues that may be impacting our sense of self-worth.

In conclusion, self-confidence is a critical component of our
well-being and success. By cultivating self-compassion,
challenging negative self-talk, setting achievable goals,
practicing self-care, and seeking support, we can build a
strong sense of self-worth and confidence. This can enable
us to navigate life's challenges with greater resilience, pursue our goals with greater determination, and live a more
fulfilling and satisfying life.

13: Overcoming Self-Doubt: Strategies for Boosting Self-Confidence

Self-doubt is a common feeling that many people experience at some point in their lives. It can be a crippling emotion that prevents us from pursuing our dreams and living our lives to the fullest. However, it is important to understand that self-doubt is a natural part of the human experience. We all have moments of insecurity and uncertainty, but it is how we respond to these feelings that determines our success in life.

In this chapter, we will explore strategies for overcoming self-doubt and boosting self-confidence. These strategies will help you develop a greater sense of self-awareness and empower you to live a more fulfilling life.

Acknowledge Your Self-Doubt

The first step in overcoming self-doubt is to acknowledge it. It is important to recognize when you are feeling doubtful or insecure about yourself or your abilities. By acknowledging your self-doubt, you can begin to address the underlying causes and take steps to overcome it.

13: OVERCOMING SELF-DOUBT: STRATEGIES FOR BOOSTING SELF-CONFIDENCE

One way to acknowledge your self-doubt is to write down your thoughts and feelings in a journal. This can help you identify patterns and triggers that contribute to your self-doubt. You can also talk to a trusted friend or therapist about your feelings, which can provide you with support and guidance.

Challenge Your Negative Thoughts

Self-doubt often stems from negative thoughts and beliefs about ourselves. These thoughts can be deeply ingrained and may be difficult to overcome. However, challenging these negative thoughts is an important step in boosting self-confidence.

One way to challenge negative thoughts is to ask yourself whether they are based in reality. Are your doubts based on actual evidence or are they simply assumptions or fears? For example, if you are doubting your ability to succeed in a new job, ask yourself whether there is any evidence to support this belief. If there is no evidence, then it may be time to challenge this negative thought and replace it with a more positive and realistic one.

13: OVERCOMING SELF-DOUBT: STRATEGIES FOR BOOSTING SELF-CONFIDENCE

Practice Self-Compassion

Self-compassion is the practice of treating ourselves with kindness, care, and understanding. It involves recognizing that we are only human and that we are not perfect. Self-compassion can help us overcome self-doubt by providing us with a sense of comfort and support.

To practice self-compassion, try treating yourself as you would treat a close friend. Be kind and understanding with yourself, and offer words of encouragement and support. You can also try practicing mindfulness, which involves being present in the moment and accepting your thoughts and feelings without judgment.

Set Realistic Goals

Setting realistic goals is an important part of building self-confidence. When we set goals that are achievable, we are more likely to succeed and feel good about ourselves. On the other hand, setting unrealistic goals can lead to feelings of failure and self-doubt.

When setting goals, be sure to make them specific, measurable, and achievable. Break larger goals down into smaller, more manageable steps, and celebrate your progress along the way. This can help you build momentum and confidence as you work towards your goals.

Take Action

Finally, taking action is perhaps the most important step in overcoming self-doubt. When we take action, we prove to ourselves that we are capable and competent. This can help build our self-confidence and provide us with a sense of accomplishment.

To take action, start by identifying small steps you can take towards your goals. These steps can be as simple as making a phone call, sending an email, or doing research. The important thing is to take action and keep moving forward, even if you feel uncertain or doubtful.

In conclusion, self-doubt is a natural part of the human experience, but it does not have to hold us back. By acknowledging our self-doubt, challenging our negative thoughts, practicing self-compassion, setting realistic goals, and taking action, we can overcome our self-doubt and boost our self-confidence.

It is important to remember that building self-confidence is a process and takes time. It may not happen overnight, but with consistent effort and practice, you can develop a greater sense of self-awareness and confidence in yourself and your abilities.

In addition to the strategies outlined above, there are other techniques and practices you can incorporate into your life to boost your self-confidence. These may include meditation, exercise, positive affirmations, and surrounding yourself with supportive people.

Ultimately, the key to overcoming self-doubt and building self-confidence is to believe in yourself and your potential. You are capable of achieving great things and living a fulfilling life. With the right mindset and tools, you can unlock your true potential and live the life you truly deserve.

14: Self-Esteem: How to Build a Positive Self-Image

Self-esteem is the foundation upon which we build our self-image, self-worth, and self-confidence. It is an essential component of our mental and emotional well-being, and it is the key to living a fulfilling life. Unfortunately, many of us struggle with low self-esteem, which can prevent us from achieving our goals, pursuing our passions, and living up to our true potential. In this chapter, we will explore what self-esteem is, why it is important, and how we can build a positive self-image.

What is self-esteem?

Self-esteem is the value and worth we place on ourselves. It is how we view ourselves, our abilities, and our place in the world. Self-esteem is not something we are born with; it is something we develop over time through our experiences, relationships, and interactions with the world around us. It can be influenced by a variety of factors, such as our upbringing, cultural and societal norms, and personal experiences.

Why is self-esteem important?

14: SELF-ESTEEM: HOW TO BUILD A POSITIVE SELF-IMAGE

Self-esteem is important because it affects our mental and emotional well-being, our relationships, and our ability to achieve our goals. When we have low self-esteem, we may feel insecure, anxious, and unhappy. We may struggle with self-doubt, fear of failure, and a lack of confidence in ourselves and our abilities. This can make it difficult to pursue our passions, take risks, and achieve our goals. On the other hand, when we have high self-esteem, we feel confident, capable, and worthy. We are more likely to take risks, pursue our passions, and achieve our goals. We are also more likely to have positive relationships with others, as we are better able to set boundaries, communicate our needs, and establish healthy connections.

How can we build a positive self-image?

Building a positive self-image takes time, effort, and self-reflection. Here are some strategies for building self-esteem and cultivating a positive self-image:

Practice self-compassion: Self-compassion is the practice of treating ourselves with kindness, understanding, and empathy. It involves acknowledging our flaws and mistakes without judgment or self-criticism. When we practice self-compassion, we are more likely to feel worthy and deserving of love and respect, which can boost our self-esteem.

Identify and challenge negative self-talk: Negative self-talk is the inner dialogue we have with ourselves that is critical, self-defeating, and unhelpful. It can be a significant barrier to building self-esteem and a positive self-image. To challenge negative self-talk, we must first become aware of it and then replace it with more positive and affirming thoughts. For example, if we find ourselves thinking, "I'm not good enough," we can challenge this thought by asking ourselves, "Is this thought true? What evidence do I have to support it?" We can then replace this thought with a more positive and affirming one, such as, "I am capable and deserving of success."

Focus on our strengths and accomplishments: We all have strengths and accomplishments, no matter how big or small. Focusing on these can help boost our self-esteem and build a more positive self-image. We can do this by keeping a gratitude journal, where we write down three things we are grateful for each day, or by making a list of our accomplishments and revisiting it when we need a confidence boost.

Practice self-care: Taking care of ourselves is an essential part of building self-esteem and a positive self-image. This includes getting enough sleep, eating a healthy diet, exercising regularly, and engaging in activities that bring us joy and fulfillment. When we take care of ourselves, we feel better both physically and mentally, which can help boost our self-esteem.

Surround ourselves with positive and supportive people: The people we surround ourselves with can have a significant impact on our self-esteem and self-image. It is important to surround ourselves with people who are positive, supportive, and uplifting. These are the people who will encourage us to pursue our goals, believe in ourselves, and challenge us to be our best selves.

Set realistic goals and celebrate our achievements: Setting realistic goals and achieving them can help build our self-esteem and confidence. It is important to set goals that are challenging but achievable and to celebrate our achievements along the way. Celebrating our achievements helps us recognize our progress and reinforces our belief in ourselves and our abilities.

Practice self-reflection: Self-reflection is the process of examining our thoughts, feelings, and behaviors to gain insight into ourselves and our experiences. It can help us identify areas where we need to grow and change and can help us cultivate a more positive self-image. We can practice self-reflection through journaling, meditation, or therapy.

In conclusion, self-esteem is essential for our mental and emotional well-being, our relationships, and our ability to achieve our goals. Building a positive self-image takes time, effort, and self-reflection. By practicing self-compassion, identifying and challenging negative self-talk, focusing on our strengths and accomplishments, practicing self-care, surrounding ourselves with positive and supportive people, setting realistic goals and celebrating our achievements, and practicing self-reflection, we can build a positive self-image and live a more fulfilling life.

15: The Power of Self-Belief: The Impact of Your Beliefs on Your Life

Introduction

Self-belief is one of the most powerful tools that you can use to achieve success in your life. It is the belief in your own abilities and the confidence that you have to take on any challenge that comes your way. The power of self-belief is often underestimated, but it can make all the difference in achieving your goals and living a fulfilling life.

In this chapter, we will explore the impact of your beliefs on your life, and how you can cultivate a strong sense of self-belief to unlock your true potential. We will examine the importance of self-belief in achieving success, the factors that influence your beliefs, and the steps you can take to strengthen your self-belief.

The Importance of Self-Belief

Self-belief is crucial for achieving success in any area of your life. Without self-belief, you may lack the confidence to pursue your goals, take risks, and face challenges. On the other hand, with a strong sense of self-belief, you can overcome obstacles, persevere in the face of adversity, and achieve your dreams.

Self-belief can also have a positive impact on your mental health and well-being. When you believe in yourself, you are more likely to feel happy, confident, and motivated. You are also more likely to experience less stress, anxiety, and depression.

The Impact of Your Beliefs

Your beliefs play a significant role in shaping your life. Your beliefs about yourself, others, and the world around you can affect your thoughts, feelings, and behaviors. Your beliefs can either support or hinder your goals and aspirations.

For example, if you believe that you are not smart enough to succeed in your career, you may be less likely to pursue promotions or opportunities for growth. Conversely, if you believe that you are capable of achieving great things, you may be more willing to take risks and pursue your goals.

Factors That Influence Your Beliefs

15: THE POWER OF SELF-BELIEF: THE IMPACT OF YOUR BELIEFS ON YOUR LIFE

Your beliefs are shaped by a variety of factors, including your upbringing, life experiences, and social environment. Your parents, teachers, and other influential figures in your life can shape your beliefs about yourself and the world around you. Your experiences can also influence your beliefs. If you have experienced failure or rejection, you may develop beliefs that you are not capable of success or that you are not worthy of love and acceptance.

Your social environment can also influence your beliefs. The messages that you receive from the media, your peers, and society as a whole can affect your beliefs about yourself and the world. For example, if you are bombarded with messages that thinness is the ideal body type, you may develop beliefs that you need to be thin to be attractive or successful.

Steps to Strengthen Your Self-Belief

Fortunately, it is possible to strengthen your self-belief. Here are some steps that you can take to cultivate a strong sense of self-belief:

Identify your limiting beliefs. The first step in strengthening your self-belief is to identify the beliefs that are holding you back. What are the beliefs that are preventing you from pursuing your goals? Write them down and examine them critically. Are they based on facts or are they simply assumptions that you have made about yourself or the world?

Challenge your limiting beliefs. Once you have identified your limiting beliefs, challenge them. Ask yourself if they are really true. Are there examples of people who have succeeded despite facing similar challenges or obstacles? What evidence do you have to support your beliefs? By questioning your beliefs, you can begin to see that they may not be as accurate or helpful as you once thought.

Cultivate a growth mindset. A growth mindset is the belief that you can develop your abilities and skills through hard work and perseverance. This mindset can help you to embrace challenges, learn from your mistakes, and see failure as an opportunity for growth. By cultivating a growth mindset, you can strengthen your self-belief and develop the confidence to pursue your goals.

Surround yourself with positivity. Your social environment can have a significant impact on your beliefs. Surround yourself with people who support and encourage you, and who have a positive outlook on life. Seek out role models who inspire you and who have achieved success in areas that you aspire to.

Practice self-care. Taking care of your physical and mental health is essential for building self-belief. Make time for activities that you enjoy and that make you feel good about yourself. Exercise regularly, eat a healthy diet, and get enough sleep. Practice mindfulness and meditation to reduce stress and improve your mental well-being.

Celebrate your successes. Celebrating your successes, no matter how small, can help to reinforce your self-belief. Take the time to acknowledge your achievements and give yourself credit for your hard work and dedication. Use your successes as evidence that you are capable of achieving your goals.

Conclusion

Self-belief is a powerful tool that can help you to achieve success and live a fulfilling life. Your beliefs about yourself, others, and the world around you can shape your thoughts, feelings, and behaviors, and can either support or hinder your goals and aspirations. By identifying your limiting beliefs, challenging them, cultivating a growth mindset, surrounding yourself with positivity, practicing self-care, and celebrating your successes, you can strengthen your self-belief and unlock your true potential. Remember, you have the power to shape your beliefs and your life.

16: Self-Identity: Understanding Who You Are and How to Define Yourself

Introduction

Self-awareness is the foundation upon which personal growth and transformation are built. To achieve true self-awareness, you must first understand who you are and how to define yourself. This chapter will explore the concept of self-identity and provide practical tools to help you gain a deeper understanding of yourself and your place in the world.

What is Self-Identity?

Self-identity refers to the beliefs, values, and characteristics that define who you are as a person. It is a multifaceted construct that includes your personality traits, attitudes, behaviors, and social roles. Self-identity is not fixed or static, but rather, it evolves over time as you encounter new experiences, challenges, and opportunities.

Why is Self-Identity Important?

16: SELF-IDENTITY: UNDERSTANDING WHO YOU ARE AND HOW TO DEFINE YOURSELF

Self-identity is important because it provides a sense of purpose, direction, and meaning in life. When you have a strong sense of self-identity, you are better equipped to make decisions that align with your values and goals, and you are more resilient in the face of adversity. Conversely, a weak sense of self-identity can lead to feelings of confusion, anxiety, and depression, and can make it difficult to navigate life's challenges.

Factors that Influence Self-Identity

There are several factors that influence self-identity, including:

Family: Your family plays a significant role in shaping your self-identity. Your parents, siblings, and extended family members teach you values, beliefs, and traditions that contribute to your sense of self.

Culture: The cultural norms, values, and beliefs of your community or society also shape your self-identity. This includes your ethnicity, religion, language, and social class.

Experiences: Your life experiences, both positive and negative, contribute to your self-identity. This includes your education, work, relationships, and hobbies.

Personality: Your personality traits, such as introversion/extroversion, openness, conscientiousness, agreeableness, and neuroticism, also play a role in shaping your self-identity.

Gender: Your gender identity, whether male, female, non-binary, or other, also influences your self-identity.

Defining Your Self-Identity

Defining your self-identity is an ongoing process that requires self-reflection, introspection, and self-awareness. Here are some steps you can take to define your self-identity:

Self-Reflection: Take time to reflect on your past experiences, values, beliefs, and goals. What has shaped your sense of self? What experiences have had the biggest impact on your life?

Identify Your Values: Your values are the principles that guide your life. They are the beliefs and ideas that you hold most dear. Identifying your values can help you make decisions that are in alignment with your true self.

Identify Your Strengths and Weaknesses: Understanding your strengths and weaknesses can help you leverage your strengths and work on improving your weaknesses.

Explore Your Passions: What are you passionate about? What activities bring you joy and fulfillment? Exploring your passions can help you identify your purpose and direction in life.

Define Your Goals: What are your short-term and long-term goals? What steps can you take to achieve those goals? Defining your goals can help you create a roadmap for your life.

Embrace Your Authentic Self: Finally, embrace your authentic self. Don't try to be someone you're not or live up to others' expectations. Be true to yourself and honor your unique qualities and strengths.

Conclusion

Self-identity is a crucial component of self-awareness and

personal growth. Understanding who you are and how to define yourself can help you live a fulfilling and meaningful life. By reflecting on your past experiences, identifying your values and strengths, exploring your passions, defining your goals, and embracing your authentic self, you can gain a deeper understanding of your self-identity and live a more authentic life.

It's important to remember that self-identity is not a fixed concept and can evolve over time. As you encounter new experiences, challenges, and opportunities, your sense of self may shift and change. Therefore, it's important to engage in ongoing self-reflection and introspection to stay in touch with your true self.

Finally, it's important to note that self-identity is a personal and unique construct. While external factors such as family, culture, and experiences can influence your sense of self, ultimately, you are the only one who can define your self-identity. Embrace your uniqueness and honor your true self, and you will be well on your way to living a fulfilling and meaningful life.

17: Self-Discovery: Exploring Your Personal Values, Goals, and Passions

Introduction

The journey towards self-awareness and personal growth begins with self-discovery. It involves exploring your personal values, goals, and passions, and understanding how they shape your identity and influence your actions. Self-discovery is a continuous process, and it requires patience, introspection, and self-reflection.

In this chapter, we will discuss the importance of self-discovery, the methods and tools you can use to explore your personal values, goals, and passions, and the benefits of doing so.

Why Self-Discovery is Important

Self-discovery is crucial for personal growth and development. It helps you understand who you are, what you stand for, and what you want to achieve in life. It enables you to make better decisions, set realistic goals, and create a fulfilling life that aligns with your values and passions.

17: SELF-DISCOVERY: EXPLORING YOUR PERSONAL VALUES, GOALS, AND PASSIONS

Without self-discovery, you may find yourself feeling lost, directionless, and unfulfilled. You may struggle with making decisions, setting goals, and finding purpose in life. Self-discovery can help you avoid these challenges and create a life that is meaningful, purposeful, and fulfilling.

Methods and Tools for Self-Discovery

There are several methods and tools you can use for self-discovery. Here are some of the most effective ones:

Self-reflection

Self-reflection involves taking the time to think about your thoughts, emotions, and behaviors. It enables you to gain insight into your inner world and understand your motivations, strengths, and weaknesses. You can practice self-reflection by journaling, meditating, or simply taking some quiet time to think.

Personality Tests

Personality tests can help you gain a better understanding of your personality traits, preferences, and tendencies. Some of the most popular personality tests include the My-

ers-Briggs Type Indicator (MBTI), the Big Five Personality
Traits, and the Enneagram.

Values Clarification Exercises

Values clarification exercises involve identifying and prioritizing your personal values. These exercises can help you understand what matters most to you and how your values influence your decisions and actions.

Goal-Setting

Goal-setting involves identifying your short-term and long-term goals and developing a plan to achieve them. Setting goals can help you focus your energy and attention, and create a sense of purpose and direction in life.

Benefits of Self-Discovery

Self-discovery can bring numerous benefits to your life. Here are some of the most important ones:

Increased Self-Awareness

Self-discovery enables you to gain a deeper understanding

of yourself and your inner world. This increased self-awareness can help you make better decisions, improve your relationships, and create a more fulfilling life.

Improved Decision-Making

Self-discovery can help you make better decisions by enabling you to understand your values, priorities, and goals. This knowledge can help you make choices that align with your true self and bring you closer to your desired outcomes.

Increased Confidence

Self-discovery can increase your confidence by helping you understand your strengths, weaknesses, and unique qualities. This knowledge can help you leverage your strengths, work on your weaknesses, and develop a sense of self-worth and self-esteem.

Greater Clarity and Direction

Self-discovery can help you gain clarity and direction in life by enabling you to identify your values, passions, and goals. This knowledge can help you create a clear vision for your future and develop a plan to achieve it.

Conclusion

Self-discovery is an essential part of personal growth and development. It enables you to understand who you are, what you stand for, and what you want to achieve in life. By exploring your personal values, goals, and passions, you can create a fulfilling life that aligns with your true self and brings you happiness and satisfaction. So take the time to reflect, identify your values and passions, and set goals that align with them. Remember that self-discovery is a continuous process, and it requires patience and dedication. But with the right tools and mindset, you can unlock your true potential and create a life that is both meaningful and fulfilling.

In the next chapter, we will discuss the importance of self-awareness and how it can help you achieve your goals and create a more fulfilling life. We will explore the different aspects of self-awareness and provide tips and strategies for cultivating it. So stay tuned for more insights and practical advice on the journey towards self-awareness and personal growth.

18: Self-Expression: How to Communicate Your Thoughts and Feelings Effectively

Introduction:

Self-expression is the art of communicating one's thoughts, feelings, and ideas effectively to others. It is an essential part of human interaction and is critical for building strong and meaningful relationships. Effective communication is the cornerstone of successful personal and professional relationships, and mastering self-expression can help you achieve your goals, both personally and professionally.

In this chapter, we will explore the importance of self-expression, the barriers that can prevent effective communication, and strategies that you can use to express yourself more effectively.

The Importance of Self-Expression:

Self-expression is essential because it allows us to share our innermost thoughts, feelings, and ideas with others. It helps us connect with others on a deeper level and builds stronger relationships. Effective communication is also critical for

18: SELF-EXPRESSION: HOW TO COMMUNICATE YOUR THOUGHTS AND FEELINGS EFFECTIVELY

success in personal and professional settings. It enables us to convey our ideas, influence others, and achieve our goals.

Self-expression is also an essential tool for personal growth and development. It allows us to explore and express our identity, values, and beliefs. When we express ourselves authentically, we feel more confident, empowered, and fulfilled.

Barriers to Effective Communication:

There are several barriers that can prevent effective communication, including:

Fear of judgment: The fear of being judged or criticized can prevent us from expressing ourselves authentically.

Lack of self-awareness: If we are not aware of our thoughts, feelings, and beliefs, it can be challenging to communicate them effectively to others.

Assumptions and stereotypes: Our assumptions and stereotypes about others can prevent us from listening to them and understanding their perspective.

18: SELF-EXPRESSION: HOW TO COMMUNICATE YOUR THOUGHTS AND FEELINGS EFFECTIVELY

Emotional barriers: Strong emotions such as anger, fear, or sadness can interfere with our ability to communicate effectively.

Language barriers: Differences in language, dialect, and cultural norms can create misunderstandings and hinder effective communication.

Strategies for Effective Self-Expression:

Here are some strategies that you can use to express yourself more effectively:

Practice active listening: Active listening involves fully engaging with the person you are communicating with, listening to their perspective, and responding thoughtfully. This helps to build trust and rapport and can create a safe space for authentic self-expression.

Build self-awareness: Develop a deeper understanding of your thoughts, feelings, and beliefs through journaling, meditation, or therapy. This will help you communicate your authentic self to others.

Use "I" statements: Using "I" statements instead of "you"

statements can help you express your thoughts and feelings without blaming or attacking others. For example, "I feel frustrated when I'm not heard" instead of "You never listen to me."

Be mindful of nonverbal communication: Nonverbal cues such as facial expressions, tone of voice, and body language can communicate more than words. Be mindful of your nonverbal cues and try to interpret others' nonverbal cues to enhance communication.

Practice empathy: Empathy involves putting yourself in someone else's shoes and understanding their perspective. Practicing empathy can help you communicate more effectively and build stronger relationships.

Conclusion:

Effective self-expression is essential for building strong and meaningful relationships, achieving personal and professional success, and personal growth and development. By identifying and overcoming barriers to effective communication and practicing strategies such as active listening, self-awareness, using "I" statements, being mindful of nonverbal communication, and practicing empathy, you can improve your self-expression skills and unlock your true potential.

19: Self-Control: Managing Your Thoughts, Emotions, and Actions

Introduction

Have you ever found yourself getting angry or upset over something that seems insignificant? Or have you ever had a hard time resisting temptation and giving in to instant gratification? These are just a few examples of situations in which self-control is necessary. Self-control, also known as self-regulation, is the ability to manage your thoughts, emotions, and actions in order to achieve your goals and lead a more fulfilling life. It is a key component of self-awareness and personal growth, and is essential for success in all aspects of life. In this chapter, we will explore the importance of self-control, the factors that influence it, and practical strategies for improving it.

The Importance of Self-Control

Self-control is important for several reasons. Firstly, it enables us to resist temptation and delay gratification. This means we can make choices that are better for us in the long run, even if they require sacrifice or effort in the short term. For example, a person with self-control may choose to save money instead of spending it on immediate pleasures, or may choose to study for an exam instead of going out with friends.

Secondly, self-control allows us to regulate our emotions. We can prevent ourselves from acting impulsively or reacting to situations in ways that may be harmful or unproductive. For example, a person with self-control may be able to avoid lashing out in anger during a disagreement or may be able to remain calm and focused during a stressful situation.

Finally, self-control is important for achieving our goals. By managing our thoughts, emotions, and actions, we can stay focused on what we want to achieve and take the necessary steps to get there. This may involve overcoming obstacles or persisting through challenges, but with self-control, we can stay motivated and committed to our goals.

Factors That Influence Self-Control

Self-control is not a fixed trait – it can be influenced by a range of factors. Some of the key factors that affect self-control include:

19: SELF-CONTROL: MANAGING YOUR THOUGHTS, EMOTIONS, AND ACTIONS

Stress: High levels of stress can impair self-control, making it harder to resist temptation or regulate our emotions.

Fatigue: Lack of sleep and mental exhaustion can also reduce self-control.

Emotional State: Our emotional state can also impact self-control. When we are feeling anxious or depressed, for example, we may find it harder to manage our thoughts and actions.

Environment: Our surroundings can also affect our self-control. For example, being in a distracting or chaotic environment can make it harder to focus and regulate our thoughts and actions.

Genetics: There is evidence to suggest that genetics play a role in self-control. Some people may be naturally more predisposed to having better self-control than others.

Improving Self-Control

Despite the factors that can influence self-control, it is a skill that can be developed and improved with practice. Here are some practical strategies for improving self-control:

Set Goals: Setting clear and specific goals can help to keep us motivated and focused. By breaking down our goals into smaller, achievable steps, we can avoid becoming overwhelmed and stay on track.

Practice Mindfulness: Mindfulness is the practice of being present and aware of our thoughts and emotions without judgment. By practicing mindfulness, we can learn to observe our thoughts and emotions without reacting impulsively to them.

Manage Stress: Taking steps to manage stress, such as exercise, meditation, or deep breathing, can help to reduce stress levels and improve self-control.

Get Enough Sleep: Getting enough sleep is essential for mental and physical health. It can also improve self-control by reducing fatigue and improving cognitive function.

Develop Healthy Habits: Developing healthy habits, such as exercise, healthy eating, and avoiding drugs and alcohol, can help to improve self-control and overall well-being.

19: SELF-CONTROL: MANAGING YOUR THOUGHTS, EMOTIONS, AND ACTIONS

Practice Self-Compassion: Practicing self-compassion means treating ourselves with kindness and understanding, especially when we experience setbacks or failures. By being kind to ourselves, we can reduce stress and anxiety, which can improve self-control.

Avoid Triggers: Identifying triggers that may lead to impulsive behavior can help us to avoid them. For example, if we know that being around certain people or in certain situations can lead to unhealthy behaviors, we can make an effort to avoid those situations.

Practice Delayed Gratification: Practicing delayed gratification means delaying immediate rewards for long-term benefits. For example, instead of eating a piece of cake immediately, we may choose to wait and eat a healthier snack later. This helps to strengthen our self-control muscles.

Seek Professional Help: If self-control issues are interfering with our daily lives, seeking professional help from a therapist or counselor can be beneficial. They can provide support and guidance in developing healthy self-control habits.

Conclusion

19: SELF-CONTROL: MANAGING YOUR THOUGHTS, EMOTIONS, AND ACTIONS

Self-control is a crucial skill for personal growth and success. It allows us to regulate our thoughts, emotions, and actions, which can help us to achieve our goals and live a more fulfilling life. While factors such as stress, fatigue, and genetics can influence self-control, there are practical strategies we can use to improve it. By setting goals, practicing mindfulness, managing stress, getting enough sleep, developing healthy habits, practicing self-compassion, avoiding triggers, practicing delayed gratification, and seeking professional help, we can strengthen our self-control muscles and unlock our true potential.

20: Self-Regulation: Techniques to Improve Self-Control and Will-power

Self-regulation is a vital skill that allows individuals to manage their impulses, emotions, and behaviors in a way that aligns with their long-term goals and values. It is a crucial aspect of self-awareness, as it requires individuals to be aware of their inner states and to make conscious choices about how they respond to different situations. Self-regulation is essential for success in all areas of life, including relationships, work, health, and personal growth. In this chapter, we will explore some techniques and strategies that can help individuals improve their self-control and will-power.

The first step in improving self-regulation is to become aware of the thoughts, feelings, and behaviors that undermine self-control. For example, many people struggle with procrastination, impulsivity, or emotional eating. By identifying these patterns, individuals can develop a plan to manage them more effectively. One way to do this is to keep a journal or diary to record thoughts, feelings, and behaviors that interfere with self-regulation. This can help individuals identify triggers and develop strategies to manage them.

Another technique to improve self-regulation is to practice mindfulness meditation. Mindfulness meditation involves focusing on the present moment and observing thoughts, emotions, and physical sensations without judgment. This practice can help individuals become more aware of their inner states and develop the ability to regulate their emotions and behaviors more effectively. Research has shown that regular mindfulness meditation can improve self-control and reduce impulsive behavior.

Physical exercise is another effective way to improve self-regulation. Regular exercise can reduce stress, improve mood, and increase self-discipline. Exercise can also help individuals build physical and mental resilience, which can improve self-control in other areas of life. Developing a regular exercise routine can be challenging, but it can be an effective way to build self-discipline and improve self-regulation.

Diet and nutrition also play a role in self-regulation. Eating a healthy, balanced diet can provide the nutrients and energy needed for optimal brain function, which can improve self-control and willpower. On the other hand, consuming large amounts of sugar or caffeine can interfere with self-regulation by increasing impulsivity and anxiety. Individuals who struggle with self-regulation may benefit from working with a nutritionist to develop a healthy eating plan that supports self-control and overall health.

Another technique to improve self-regulation is to set specific goals and develop a plan to achieve them. Research has shown that individuals who set specific, challenging goals are more likely to achieve them than those who have vague or unrealistic goals. Developing a plan to achieve goals can also help individuals stay on track and manage distractions and obstacles more effectively. It is important to break down larger goals into smaller, achievable steps to build momentum and stay motivated.

Developing a strong support network is also important for improving self-regulation. Having friends, family, or a mentor who can offer encouragement, feedback, and accountability can help individuals stay focused and motivated. Joining a support group or working with a coach or therapist can also provide valuable guidance and support in developing self-regulation skills.

Finally, it is important to practice self-compassion and for-giveness when working on self-regulation. It is natural to experience setbacks and obstacles when trying to improve self-control, and it is important to be kind and patient with oneself during these times. Rather than beating oneself up for mistakes or failures, it is important to learn from them and use them as opportunities for growth and improve-ment.

In conclusion, self-regulation is a vital skill that allows indi-viduals to manage their impulses, emotions, and behaviors in a way that aligns with their long-term goals and values. There are many techniques and strategies that individuals can use to improve self-control and willpower, including mindfulness meditation, exercise, diet and nutrition, goal-setting, developing a support network, and practicing self-compassion and forgiveness. By practicing these techniques and incorporating them into daily life, individuals can im-prove their self-regulation skills and achieve greater success in all areas of life.

It is important to note that improving self-regulation is a

continuous process that requires ongoing effort and practice. It is not a quick fix or a one-time solution, but rather a
lifelong journey of self-discovery and personal growth. By
remaining committed to the process and embracing the ups
and downs of the journey, individuals can develop a strong
sense of self-awareness, self-control, and inner peace.

One of the key benefits of improving self-regulation is that it
can lead to greater resilience in the face of challenges and
adversity. When individuals are able to regulate their emotions and behaviors, they are better able to cope with stress
and bounce back from setbacks. This resilience can help individuals achieve greater success and fulfillment in all areas
of life, from personal relationships to professional endeavors.

In addition to improving resilience, self-regulation can also
lead to greater happiness and well-being. When individuals
are able to manage their thoughts, emotions, and behaviors
in a way that aligns with their values and goals, they experience a greater sense of inner peace and contentment. This
sense of well-being can enhance relationships, boost creativity and productivity, and lead to a more fulfilling life

overall.

In conclusion, self-regulation is a crucial aspect of self-awareness and personal growth. By developing self-control and willpower, individuals can manage their impulses, emotions, and behaviors in a way that aligns with their long-term goals and values. Through techniques such as mindfulness meditation, exercise, diet and nutrition, goal-setting, developing a support network, and practicing self-compassion and forgiveness, individuals can improve their self-regulation skills and achieve greater success, resilience, and well-being in all areas of life.

21: Self-Motivation: Strategies to Stay Focused and Driven

Introduction

Self-motivation is the foundation of achieving success in every area of our lives. It is the driving force that propels us towards our goals and helps us stay focused on our vision. The ability to self-motivate is especially crucial in today's world, where we are constantly bombarded with distractions and faced with countless choices.

In this chapter, we will explore some strategies that can help us cultivate self-motivation and maintain focus on our goals. These strategies are practical, easy to implement, and have been proven to work in various fields of endeavor.

The Power of Self-Motivation

Self-motivation is the ability to generate the necessary drive, energy, and enthusiasm to take action towards a desired outcome. It is an internal force that inspires us to pursue our goals despite the challenges we may encounter along the way.

Self-motivation is a powerful force that has driven many

successful people to achieve their dreams. It is the key to unlocking our true potential and living a fulfilling life. Without self-motivation, we are likely to be passive, lack focus, and easily give up on our goals.

The good news is that self-motivation can be developed and strengthened over time with practice and dedication. The following strategies will help you cultivate self-motivation and stay focused on your goals.

Strategy #1: Set Clear Goals

One of the most important steps towards self-motivation is setting clear and specific goals. When we have a clear idea of what we want to achieve, it becomes easier to focus our energy and take action towards our desired outcome.

Setting clear goals involves identifying what we want to achieve, why it is important to us, and how we plan to achieve it. Goals should be specific, measurable, and achievable within a reasonable timeframe.

For example, if your goal is to start a business, you might set a specific target such as "I want to launch my business within the next six months and generate $50,000 in revenue within the first year." This specific goal gives you a clear target to work towards and helps you stay focused on the actions needed to achieve it.

Strategy #2: Build a Positive Mindset

A positive mindset is essential for self-motivation. It helps us stay focused on our goals and enables us to overcome obstacles and setbacks along the way. Developing a positive mindset involves cultivating positive thoughts and beliefs, and focusing on the opportunities and possibilities that exist.

To build a positive mindset, it is important to practice gratitude, affirmations, and visualization. These practices help us focus on the positive aspects of our lives and envision a future where our goals are achieved.

Gratitude involves acknowledging and appreciating the good things in our lives. It helps us develop a sense of abundance and optimism, which are essential for self-motivation. Affirmations involve repeating positive statements about ourselves and our goals, which help us stay focused on our desired outcome. Visualization involves mentally picturing ourselves achieving our goals, which helps us stay motivated and focused on taking action towards our desired outcome.

Strategy #3: Break Down Tasks into Smaller Steps

Breaking down tasks into smaller steps is a useful strategy for staying motivated and focused on our goals. When we face a large task or project, it can be overwhelming and difficult to know where to start. Breaking it down into smaller steps makes it more manageable and helps us stay motivated as we see progress being made.

To break down tasks into smaller steps, start by identifying the main components of the task or project. Then, break each component down into smaller, more manageable tasks. Finally, schedule each task into your calendar, giving yourself enough time to complete each step.

For example, if your goal is to write a book, you might break the task down into smaller steps such as outlining the book, researching the topic, writing the first chapter, editing the first chapter, and so on. By breaking the task down into smaller steps, you can see progress being made and stay motivated as you move closer to your goal.

Strategy #4: Create a Supportive Environment

The environment we create around us can have a significant impact on our motivation and ability to achieve our goals. Creating a supportive environment involves surrounding ourselves with people who share our goals and values, as well as creating a physical environment that supports our productivity and motivation.

To create a supportive environment, start by identifying the people in your life who support your goals and values. Seek out their company and engage in activities that align with your goals. You can also join groups or organizations that share your interests and values.

Creating a physical environment that supports your motivation and productivity involves eliminating distractions and creating a workspace that is conducive to focused work. This might involve minimizing clutter, adding plants or other natural elements to your workspace, and ensuring that your workspace is well-lit and comfortable.

Strategy #5: Practice Self-Care

Self-care is an essential component of self-motivation. When we take care of ourselves, we have the energy and mental clarity to focus on our goals and take action towards our desired outcome. Practicing self-care involves taking care of our physical, emotional, and mental well-being.

To practice self-care, start by prioritizing sleep, exercise, and nutrition. These three components are essential for maintaining physical health and energy levels. It is also important to prioritize activities that bring us joy and relaxation, such as spending time with loved ones, reading, or engaging in hobbies.

In addition to physical self-care, it is important to prioritize emotional and mental self-care. This might involve engaging in mindfulness practices, seeking therapy or counseling when needed, and engaging in activities that promote self-reflection and personal growth.

Conclusion

Self-motivation is a critical component of achieving success in every area of our lives. By setting clear goals, building a positive mindset, breaking down tasks into smaller steps, creating a supportive environment, and practicing self-care, we can cultivate self-motivation and stay focused on our goals.

Remember, self-motivation is a skill that can be developed and strengthened over time with practice and dedication. By incorporating these strategies into your daily life, you can unlock your true potential and achieve your goals with confidence and focus.

22: Self-Discipline: Developing Habits for Success and Personal Growth

Self-discipline is the foundation upon which every successful life is built. It is the ability to make choices that are in line with your goals and values, even when those choices are difficult or uncomfortable. Self-discipline is what allows you to get up early in the morning to go for a run, even when you'd rather hit the snooze button; it's what keeps you focused on your work when you'd rather be scrolling through social media; and it's what enables you to make healthy food choices when you're tempted by junk food.

In this chapter, we will explore the concept of self-discipline and how to develop habits that will help you cultivate it. We will cover a range of topics, including the benefits of self-discipline, the science behind habit formation, and practical tips for developing self-discipline in your own life.

Why Self-Discipline Matters

Self-discipline is important for a number of reasons. First and foremost, it allows you to achieve your goals. When you have the ability to stay focused and stay on track, you can accomplish anything you set your mind to. Additionally, self-discipline can help you maintain healthy habits, both physically and mentally. When you have the ability to make choices that support your well-being, you are more likely to feel good and perform well in all areas of your life.

In contrast, lack of self-discipline can lead to a range of negative outcomes. When you are unable to resist temptations or make healthy choices, you may experience negative consequences, such as poor health, financial problems, and relationship issues. Additionally, lack of self-discipline can lead to feelings of guilt, shame, and self-doubt, which can impact your mental health and overall well-being.

The Science of Habit Formation

Before we dive into practical tips for developing self-discipline, it's important to understand the science behind habit formation. Habits are automatic behaviors that are triggered by specific cues, such as a particular time of day or a certain location. When you repeat a behavior in response to a cue enough times, it becomes a habit that is deeply ingrained in your brain.

22: SELF-DISCIPLINE: DEVELOPING HABITS FOR SUCCESS AND PERSONAL GROWTH

The key to forming new habits is to create a strong association between the cue and the behavior you want to adopt. For example, if you want to start exercising every morning, you might choose to do your workout at the same time every day and in the same location. This will help your brain associate that time and location with exercise, making it easier to stick to your new habit.

Tips for Developing Self-Discipline

Now that we understand the science behind habit formation, let's explore some practical tips for developing self-discipline:

Set Clear Goals

The first step in developing self-discipline is to set clear goals for yourself. When you have a specific outcome in mind, you are more likely to stay motivated and focused on your goal. Make sure your goals are realistic, measurable, and aligned with your values.

Create a Plan

Once you have set your goals, it's important to create a plan for achieving them. Break your goals down into smaller, manageable steps, and create a timeline for completing each step. Having a clear plan in place will help you stay on track and avoid feeling overwhelmed.

Find an Accountability Partner

Having someone to hold you accountable can be a powerful motivator for developing self-discipline. Find a friend or family member who shares your goals and is willing to support you along the way. Check in with each other regularly to share progress and offer encouragement.

Practice Mindfulness

Practicing mindfulness can help you develop greater self-awareness and strengthen your ability to make conscious choices. When you are more aware of your thoughts and emotions, you can more easily recognize when you are tempted to make choices that don't align with your goals and values. Take time each day to practice mindfulness through activities like meditation, deep breathing, or simply paying attention to your surroundings.

22: SELF-DISCIPLINE: DEVELOPING HABITS FOR SUCCESS AND PERSONAL GROWTH

Remove Temptations

One of the keys to developing self-discipline is to remove temptations from your environment. This might mean getting rid of junk food in your pantry, unfollowing social media accounts that trigger negative emotions, or avoiding situations that tend to lead to unhealthy choices. By removing temptations, you reduce the likelihood of giving in to them.

Start Small

Developing self-discipline is a process, and it's important to start small. Choose one habit to focus on at a time, and make small changes to your behavior to support that habit. For example, if you want to start meditating every day, start with just a few minutes a day and gradually increase the amount of time you spend meditating.

Celebrate Your Progress

Finally, it's important to celebrate your progress along the way. Acknowledge and celebrate small wins, like completing a workout or making a healthy meal choice. Celebrating your progress can help keep you motivated and reinforce the importance of your goals.

Conclusion

Developing self-discipline is a key component of personal growth and success. By understanding the science of habit formation and implementing practical tips for developing self-discipline, you can cultivate the habits necessary to achieve your goals and live a fulfilling life. Remember to set clear goals, create a plan, find an accountability partner, practice mindfulness, remove temptations, start small, and celebrate your progress. With dedication and perseverance, you can develop the self-discipline necessary to unlock your true potential and live your best life.

23: Self-Management: Balancing Your Personal and Professional Life

Self-management is one of the essential components of self-awareness. It refers to the ability to manage your emotions, thoughts, and behaviors to achieve your goals effectively. Self-management is critical in both personal and professional life as it helps you maintain a healthy work-life balance, which is essential for your overall well-being. In this chapter, we will discuss how you can balance your personal and professional life through self-management.

Self-Management in Professional Life

In today's fast-paced and competitive world, work-life balance has become a significant concern for many individuals. The pressure to meet deadlines, achieve targets, and maintain productivity can take a toll on your mental and physical health. Therefore, self-management is crucial in the professional sphere to help you maintain a healthy work-life balance.

One way to manage your professional life is to set realistic goals and prioritize them accordingly. Setting achievable goals can help you stay motivated and focused, and prioritizing them can help you manage your time effectively. Additionally, learning to say no to tasks that do not align with your goals or values can help you avoid burnout and stress.

Another crucial aspect of self-management in the professional sphere is time management. Effective time management involves scheduling your tasks and activities in a way that maximizes your productivity and minimizes stress. You can use tools such as calendars, to-do lists, and reminders to help you manage your time effectively.

Self-Management in Personal Life

Self-management is not limited to the professional sphere but is equally important in your personal life. Balancing your personal and professional life is crucial for your overall well-being and happiness. Therefore, self-management in your personal life involves developing healthy habits and routines that help you achieve your personal goals and maintain a healthy lifestyle.

One way to manage your personal life is to set realistic and achievable goals. Setting personal goals can help you stay motivated and focused on your priorities. Additionally, prioritizing your goals can help you manage your time effectively, which is essential in balancing your personal and professional life.

Another crucial aspect of self-management in your personal life is developing healthy habits and routines. Habits such as regular exercise, healthy eating, and getting enough sleep can help you maintain a healthy lifestyle and improve your overall well-being. Additionally, developing a routine can help you manage your time effectively, which is essential in balancing your personal and professional life.

Balancing Your Personal and Professional Life

Balancing your personal and professional life is essential for your overall well-being and happiness. However, achieving this balance can be challenging, especially in today's fast-paced and competitive world. Therefore, self-management is critical in balancing your personal and professional life.

One way to balance your personal and professional life is to set boundaries. Setting boundaries can help you avoid burnout and stress by preventing work from encroaching on your personal life. For instance, you can set specific times for work-related activities and avoid checking your work emails or taking work calls outside of those times.

Another way to balance your personal and professional life is to practice self-care. Self-care involves taking care of your physical, mental, and emotional health. Self-care activities such as meditation, yoga, and spending time with loved ones can help you reduce stress and improve your overall well-being.

Conclusion

Self-management is crucial in both personal and professional life. It involves managing your emotions, thoughts, and behaviors to achieve your goals effectively. In the professional sphere, self-management involves setting realistic goals, prioritizing tasks, and managing your time effectively. In your personal life, self-management involves developing healthy habits and routines and setting boundaries to balance your personal and professional life. By practicing self-management, you can achieve a healthy work-life balance, which is essential for your overall well-being and happiness.

24: Self-Direction: How to Set Goals and Achieve Them

Self-Direction: How to Set Goals and Achieve Them

Self-awareness is about more than just understanding your emotions and thought patterns. It's also about setting goals and working towards them with purpose and intention. Setting and achieving goals is a critical aspect of personal growth and transformation, and it requires self-direction.

Self-direction is the ability to set goals for yourself and take the necessary steps to achieve them. It's about taking responsibility for your life and actively pursuing your dreams and ambitions. In this chapter, we will explore the importance of self-direction, how to set goals effectively, and how to achieve them.

The Importance of Self-Direction

Self-direction is crucial to achieving personal and professional success. It's the key to turning your dreams into reality and living a fulfilling life. Without self-direction, you'll find yourself drifting through life without a clear purpose or direction.

24: SELF-DIRECTION: HOW TO SET GOALS AND ACHIEVE THEM

Self-direction allows you to take control of your life and make the most of your potential. When you have a clear direction and purpose, you'll be more motivated, focused, and productive. You'll also be better equipped to deal with challenges and setbacks along the way.

How to Set Goals Effectively

Setting goals is an essential step towards achieving success and living a fulfilling life. However, setting goals is more than just writing down a list of things you want to accomplish. Effective goal setting requires careful planning, realistic expectations, and a clear understanding of what you want to achieve.

Here are some steps to help you set goals effectively:

Identify Your Values and Priorities

Before you start setting goals, it's essential to identify your values and priorities. Ask yourself what matters most to you in life and what you want to achieve. Make a list of your core values and use them as a guide for setting your goals.

Define Your Goals

24: SELF-DIRECTION: HOW TO SET GOALS AND ACHIEVE THEM

Once you've identified your values and priorities, it's time to define your goals. Be specific about what you want to achieve and why it matters to you. Write your goals down and make sure they're measurable, achievable, and realistic.

Create a Plan

Once you've defined your goals, create a plan for achieving them. Break your goals down into smaller, manageable steps, and set deadlines for each one. Make sure your plan is realistic and takes into account any obstacles or challenges you may face along the way.

Take Action

With your plan in place, it's time to take action. Start working towards your goals by taking the first step. Keep track of your progress and adjust your plan as needed. Stay motivated and focused by reminding yourself of why your goals matter to you.

How to Achieve Your Goals

Setting goals is only the first step towards achieving success. To turn your goals into reality, you need to take action and stay committed to the process. Here are some tips for achieving your goals:

Stay Focused

Stay focused on your goals by keeping them at the forefront of your mind. Visualize yourself achieving your goals and imagine how it will feel. Remind yourself of your goals regularly and stay committed to the process.

Stay Motivated

Stay motivated by celebrating your progress along the way. Take time to acknowledge your achievements and the hard work you've put in. Surround yourself with people who support and encourage you, and don't be afraid to ask for help when you need it.

Stay Flexible

Stay flexible by being open to change and adjusting your plan as needed. Be prepared to face challenges and setbacks along the way, and don't be afraid to try new approaches. Stay focused on your goals, but be willing to adapt your plan to achieve them.

24: SELF-DIRECTION: HOW TO SET GOALS AND ACHIEVE THEM

Stay Committed

Stay committed to the process by staying true to your values and priorities. Don't give up when things get tough, and don't let setbacks or failures deter you from pursuing your goals. Keep pushing forward, and remember why your goals matter to you.

Stay Accountable

Stay accountable by tracking your progress and holding yourself responsible for achieving your goals. Keep a record of your successes and challenges, and evaluate your progress regularly. If you find yourself falling behind, don't be afraid to adjust your plan or seek help from others.

Stay Positive

Stay positive by focusing on the progress you've made and the opportunities that lie ahead. Don't get discouraged by setbacks or obstacles, and don't compare your progress to others. Stay confident in your abilities and believe in yourself and your goals.

Conclusion

24: SELF-DIRECTION: HOW TO SET GOALS AND ACHIEVE THEM

Self-direction is a crucial aspect of personal growth and transformation. It's the key to setting and achieving goals that matter to you and living a fulfilling life. By identifying your values and priorities, defining your goals, creating a plan, taking action, staying focused, motivated, flexible, committed, accountable, and positive, you can unlock your true potential and achieve the success you deserve. Remember that self-direction is a process, and it takes time and effort to achieve your goals. Stay patient, stay committed, and enjoy the journey.

25: Self-Actualization: Living Your Best Life and Achieving Your Dreams

Self-actualization is the process of realizing your full potential and achieving your dreams. It's about living your best life and becoming the person you were meant to be. Self-actualization is a lifelong journey that requires a deep understanding of yourself, your strengths, weaknesses, values, and beliefs. It also involves setting goals, taking action, and continuously learning and growing.

In this chapter, we will explore the concept of self-actualization in more detail and discuss the steps you can take to live your best life and achieve your dreams.

What is Self-Actualization?

Self-actualization is a term that was first introduced by Abraham Maslow, a psychologist who believed that humans have an innate drive to realize their full potential. Maslow identified self-actualization as the highest level of human needs in his hierarchy of needs. According to Maslow, once our basic physiological and safety needs are met, we strive to fulfill our psychological needs, such as the need for love and belonging, self-esteem, and self-actualization.

Self-actualization is a complex concept that encompasses many different aspects of human experience, including creativity, spirituality, morality, and the search for meaning and purpose in life. Self-actualized individuals are characterized by a strong sense of self-awareness, authenticity, and autonomy. They are able to express their true selves and live according to their values and beliefs, rather than conforming to societal expectations or external pressures.

The Benefits of Self-Actualization

Self-actualization is not only a fulfilling and rewarding process, but it also has many benefits for our mental and physical health. Studies have shown that self-actualized individuals are more resilient, have better coping skills, and experience less stress and anxiety. They are also more likely to have positive relationships, a sense of purpose and meaning in life, and a higher level of overall well-being.

Steps to Achieving Self-Actualization

Self-actualization is a process that requires self-reflection, self-awareness, and a willingness to learn and grow. Here are some steps you can take to achieve self-actualization and live your best life:

Identify Your Values and Beliefs

The first step in achieving self-actualization is to identify your core values and beliefs. These are the principles and ideals that guide your life and define who you are as a person. Take some time to reflect on what is most important to you, what motivates you, and what you stand for. Once you have a clear understanding of your values and beliefs, you can use them as a compass to guide your decisions and actions.

Set Goals and Take Action

Once you have identified your values and beliefs, it's important to set goals that align with them. These goals should be specific, measurable, and realistic. Break them down into smaller steps and create a plan of action to achieve them. Taking action towards your goals is essential for achieving self-actualization, as it helps you develop a sense of competence, accomplishment, and personal growth.

25: SELF-ACTUALIZATION: LIVING YOUR BEST LIFE AND ACHIEVING YOUR DREAMS

Develop Self-Awareness

Self-awareness is the foundation of self-actualization. It involves being aware of your thoughts, feelings, and behaviors, and understanding how they influence your life. Developing self-awareness requires practice and self-reflection. Pay attention to your thoughts and emotions, and try to identify patterns or triggers that may be holding you back. Journaling, meditation, and therapy are all effective ways to develop self-awareness.

Embrace Your Authentic Self

Self-actualized individuals are authentic and true to themselves. They are able to express their true selves and live according to their values and beliefs, rather than conforming to societal expectations or external pressures. Embracing your authentic self requires self-acceptance and self-love. It means acknowledging your strengths and weaknesses, being comfortable with who you are, and not trying to be someone else. When you embrace your authentic self, you can live a more fulfilling and satisfying life, as you are no longer trying to live up to someone else's expectations.

25: SELF-ACTUALIZATION: LIVING YOUR BEST LIFE AND ACHIEVING YOUR DREAMS

Cultivate Creativity and Curiosity

Self-actualized individuals are often creative and curious. They have a strong desire to learn, explore, and try new things. Cultivating creativity and curiosity can help you develop new skills and perspectives, and can also provide a sense of joy and fulfillment. Try taking up a new hobby, learning a new skill, or exploring a new place.

Find Meaning and Purpose in Life

Self-actualized individuals have a strong sense of meaning and purpose in life. They feel that their life has significance and that they are contributing to something greater than themselves. Finding meaning and purpose in life requires self-reflection and exploration. Ask yourself what you are passionate about, what gives you a sense of fulfillment, and how you can contribute to the world in a meaningful way.

Practice Mindfulness and Gratitude

Mindfulness and gratitude are important practices for achieving self-actualization. Mindfulness involves being present in the moment and fully engaged in your experiences. It can help you develop a greater sense of awareness and appreciation for the world around you. Gratitude involves focusing on the positive aspects of your life and expressing gratitude for them. It can help you cultivate a more positive and optimistic outlook on life.

In conclusion, self-actualization is a lifelong journey that requires self-reflection, self-awareness, and a willingness to learn and grow. By identifying your values and beliefs, setting goals and taking action, developing self-awareness, embracing your authentic self, cultivating creativity and curiosity, finding meaning and purpose in life, and practicing mindfulness and gratitude, you can achieve self-actualization and live your best life. Remember, self-actualization is not a destination, but a journey. Enjoy the process and embrace the challenges and opportunities that come your way.

26: Self-Transformation: How to Change Your Life for the Better

Self-Transformation: How to Change Your Life for the Better

Self-transformation is the process of improving oneself in various aspects of life to achieve personal growth and development. It involves a conscious effort to make positive changes in your life, which can lead to a better quality of life and increased well-being. In this chapter, we will explore how to transform your life for the better and achieve your full potential.

The Importance of Self-Transformation

Self-transformation is important for personal growth and development. It allows you to become the best version of yourself and achieve your full potential. When you transform yourself, you can improve your physical, emotional, and mental health, enhance your relationships, and increase your overall happiness and well-being.

Self-transformation is also essential in the modern world, where we face various challenges, including stress, anxiety, and burnout. By transforming yourself, you can develop resilience, adaptability, and coping skills, which can help you navigate the challenges of the modern world.

Steps to Self-Transformation

Self-transformation is a gradual process that requires commitment, effort, and persistence. Here are some steps you can take to transform yourself for the better:

Define Your Goals and Values

The first step in self-transformation is to define your goals and values. Identify what is important to you and what you want to achieve in life. Write down your goals and break them down into smaller, achievable steps.

Identify Your Strengths and Weaknesses

To transform yourself, you need to identify your strengths and weaknesses. This will help you leverage your strengths and work on your weaknesses. Take a personality test or seek feedback from others to gain a better understanding of your strengths and weaknesses.

26: SELF-TRANSFORMATION: HOW TO CHANGE YOUR LIFE FOR THE BETTER

Develop Self-Awareness

Self-awareness is the foundation of self-transformation. It involves being mindful of your thoughts, feelings, and behaviors. Practice mindfulness meditation, journaling, or therapy to develop self-awareness.

Create a Plan of Action

Once you have defined your goals, identified your strengths and weaknesses, and developed self-awareness, create a plan of action. Set specific, measurable, achievable, relevant, and time-bound (SMART) goals and develop a plan to achieve them.

Take Action

The next step in self-transformation is to take action. Follow your plan of action and take small steps towards your goals every day. Celebrate your progress and adjust your plan if necessary.

Develop Resilience

Self-transformation involves facing challenges and setbacks.

26: SELF-TRANSFORMATION: HOW TO CHANGE YOUR LIFE FOR THE BETTER

To develop resilience, cultivate a growth mindset, practice self-compassion, and develop coping skills.

Seek Support

Self-transformation can be a challenging journey. Seek support from friends, family, or a therapist. Join a support group or seek mentorship to gain inspiration and guidance.

Self-Transformation Techniques

Here are some self-transformation techniques you can practice to transform yourself for the better:

Mindfulness Meditation

Mindfulness meditation involves focusing your attention on the present moment and observing your thoughts and feelings without judgment. It can help you develop self-awareness and reduce stress and anxiety.

Positive Affirmations

Positive affirmations are statements that reinforce positive beliefs and values. They can help you develop a positive mindset and overcome negative self-talk.

Gratitude Practice

Gratitude practice involves focusing on the positive aspects of your life and expressing gratitude for them. It can help you develop a positive outlook and increase your overall well-being.

Journaling

Journaling involves writing down your thoughts, feelings, and experiences. It can help you develop self-awareness, process your emotions, and gain insight into your life.

Exercise

Exercise can help you improve your physical and mental health. It can reduce stress and anxiety, improve sleep, and increase your energy and mood. Find an exercise routine that you enjoy and commit to it regularly.

Healthy Eating

Healthy eating involves consuming a balanced diet that

provides your body with the necessary nutrients. Avoid processed and unhealthy foods, and focus on whole foods, fruits, vegetables, and lean proteins.

Learn a New Skill

Learning a new skill can help you develop new interests, improve your self-confidence, and expand your horizons. Choose a skill that interests you and commit to learning it regularly.

Practice Self-Care

Self-care involves taking care of your physical, emotional, and mental health. Practice self-care regularly by getting enough sleep, taking breaks when needed, and engaging in activities that bring you joy and relaxation.

Benefits of Self-Transformation

Self-transformation can have numerous benefits, including:

Improved Mental and Emotional Health

Self-transformation can help you develop self-awareness,

cultivate a positive mindset, and manage stress and anxiety. It can also improve your emotional regulation and increase your overall well-being.

Increased Self-Confidence

Self-transformation can help you identify your strengths and work on your weaknesses. This can increase your self-confidence and self-esteem.

Better Relationships

Self-transformation can improve your communication skills, increase your empathy and understanding, and enhance your relationships with others.

Increased Productivity

Self-transformation can help you develop better time management skills, increase your motivation, and improve your focus and concentration. This can increase your productivity and help you achieve your goals.

Greater Fulfillment

26: SELF-TRANSFORMATION: HOW TO CHANGE YOUR LIFE FOR THE BETTER

Self-transformation can help you identify your values and purpose in life. This can lead to a greater sense of fulfillment and satisfaction.

Conclusion

Self-transformation is a gradual process that requires commitment, effort, and persistence. It involves defining your goals and values, identifying your strengths and weaknesses, developing self-awareness, creating a plan of action, taking action, developing resilience, and seeking support. By practicing self-transformation techniques and incorporating them into your daily life, you can achieve personal growth and development, and live a fulfilling life in the modern world.

27: Self-Growth: Strategies to Continuously Improve Yourself

Self-growth: Strategies to Continuously Improve Yourself

Self-growth is an ongoing process that requires constant attention and effort. It's the journey towards personal development, where you become the best version of yourself. It's a continuous process that requires patience, perseverance, and a willingness to learn and adapt.

In this chapter, we will discuss strategies that you can use to continuously improve yourself. These strategies are not a one-size-fits-all solution, but rather a starting point for you to develop your own unique path towards self-growth.

Develop a Growth Mindset

One of the most critical strategies to improve yourself is developing a growth mindset. A growth mindset is the belief that your abilities can be developed through dedication and hard work. This mindset encourages you to embrace challenges, learn from criticism, and persist in the face of setbacks.

To develop a growth mindset, you need to focus on your effort rather than your innate abilities. Celebrate your progress, even if it's slow. Embrace challenges, and don't be afraid to fail. Instead, see failure as an opportunity to learn and grow. Remember, growth is a process, not a destination.

Set Clear Goals

Another strategy to improve yourself is setting clear and specific goals. Goals give you direction and focus, which are essential for self-growth. When setting goals, make sure they are achievable, measurable, and realistic. Break them down into smaller, more manageable tasks, and create a timeline for completion.

Goal setting is not just about achieving what you want. It's also about discovering what you're capable of and pushing yourself to new heights. When you achieve your goals, take time to reflect on what you learned and how you can apply it to future endeavors.

Create a Personal Development Plan

A personal development plan is a roadmap that outlines

your goals, strategies, and actions for self-growth. It's a comprehensive plan that includes everything from improving your skills to building your network and achieving your goals.

To create a personal development plan, start by assessing your strengths and weaknesses. Identify areas where you want to improve, and set specific goals for each area. Then, develop strategies to achieve those goals, such as taking courses, attending workshops, or seeking mentorship.

Your personal development plan should be dynamic and adaptable. Review it regularly and make changes as needed to ensure you stay on track.

Learn Continuously

Learning is a lifelong process that never ends. To improve yourself continuously, you need to be willing to learn and acquire new knowledge and skills. Seek out opportunities to learn, such as taking courses, reading books, attending workshops, or seeking mentorship.

Learning doesn't have to be formal or structured. It can also be informal, such as learning from experience, experimenting, or seeking feedback. The key is to be curious, open-minded, and willing to explore new ideas and perspectives.

Build a Support System

Self-growth is not a solo journey. It's essential to have a support system of people who encourage, motivate, and challenge you to be your best self. Your support system can include family, friends, mentors, coaches, or peers.

When building your support system, choose people who share your values and goals. Seek out individuals who can provide constructive feedback, hold you accountable, and offer guidance and support when needed.

Practice Self-Care

Self-growth also involves taking care of yourself physically, mentally, and emotionally. Practicing self-care means making time for activities that rejuvenate and nourish your mind, body, and soul.

Self-care activities can include exercise, meditation, journaling, reading, spending time in nature, or simply relaxing.

27: SELF-GROWTH: STRATEGIES TO CONTINUOUSLY IMPROVE YOURSELF

The key is to prioritize your well-being and make self-care a non-negotiable part of your routine.

Embrace Change

Change is inevitable, and it's essential to embrace it if you want to continuously improve yourself. Instead of resisting change, embrace it as an opportunity for growth and development.

To embrace change, start by acknowledging and accepting that it's a natural part of life. Focus on the opportunities that come with change, rather than the challenges. When faced with a change, look for ways to adapt and learn from the experience.

Remember, change can be uncomfortable, but it's necessary for personal growth. Embrace it, and you'll find that you can achieve more than you ever thought possible.

Practice Gratitude

Gratitude is a powerful tool for personal growth. It helps you appreciate what you have and focus on the positive aspects of your life. Gratitude also fosters a sense of well-being and can improve your mental health.

To practice gratitude, start by taking time each day to reflect on what you're thankful for. Write down three things you're grateful for, no matter how small they may seem. This simple practice can help shift your mindset from one of scarcity to abundance.

Gratitude can also be expressed to others. Take time to thank those who have helped you along your journey. Acknowledge their contributions and let them know how much you appreciate them.

Take Risks

Taking risks is essential for personal growth. It means stepping out of your comfort zone and trying something new or different. When you take risks, you stretch yourself and challenge your limits, which can lead to personal growth and development.

To take risks, start by identifying areas where you feel stuck or stagnant. Look for opportunities to try something new or different. Start small, and gradually work your way up to bigger risks.

Remember, taking risks doesn't mean being reckless. It means being willing to try something new or different, even if it's outside your comfort zone. When you take risks, you'll find that you can achieve more than you ever thought possible.

Celebrate Your Successes

Finally, it's essential to celebrate your successes along your journey of self-growth. Celebrating your successes helps you recognize and appreciate your progress, which can boost your confidence and motivation.

When you achieve a goal or milestone, take time to celebrate your success. Acknowledge your hard work and dedication, and reflect on what you've learned along the way. Celebrate with others who have supported you along your journey, and use this momentum to propel yourself forward towards your next goal.

Conclusion

Self-growth is a lifelong journey that requires constant attention and effort. By adopting the strategies outlined in this chapter, you can continuously improve yourself and unlock your true potential. Remember, self-growth is not a one-size-fits-all solution. It's a personalized journey that requires patience, perseverance, and a willingness to learn and adapt. Embrace the journey, and you'll find that you can achieve more than you ever thought possible.

28: Self-Empowerment: Taking Charge of Your Life and Making Positive Changes

Self-empowerment is about taking control of your life, making positive changes, and becoming the best version of yourself. It is the process of discovering your true potential, unlocking your inner strength, and creating a fulfilling life in the modern world. In this chapter, we will explore the key elements of self-empowerment, including self-awareness, self-confidence, self-belief, and self-motivation. We will also provide practical tips and strategies for building self-empowerment and achieving your goals.

Self-awareness is the foundation of self-empowerment. It is the ability to recognize your strengths and weaknesses, your values and beliefs, and your emotions and behaviors. Self-awareness allows you to understand who you are, what you want, and how you can achieve your goals. It helps you to identify your passions, talents, and interests and to make decisions that align with your values and purpose.

To build self-awareness, it is essential to practice mindfulness, meditation, and reflection. Mindfulness is the practice of being present and aware of your thoughts, feelings, and sensations without judgment. Meditation is the practice of focusing your attention on a specific object or thought to achieve mental clarity and relaxation. Reflection is the process of introspection, where you examine your thoughts and experiences to gain insight into your behaviors and beliefs.

Self-confidence is another critical element of self-empowerment. It is the belief in your abilities, skills, and talents. Self-confidence allows you to take risks, overcome challenges, and pursue your dreams with determination and resilience. It also helps you to build positive relationships, communicate effectively, and assert yourself in a respectful and confident manner.

To build self-confidence, it is essential to focus on your strengths, set achievable goals, and practice self-compassion. You can also build self-confidence by taking small steps towards your goals, celebrating your achievements, and surrounding yourself with positive and supportive people.

Self-belief is the conviction that you can achieve your goals and succeed in life. It is the belief that you have the potential to create the life you want and to overcome any obstacles that come your way. Self-belief allows you to maintain a positive attitude, persevere through setbacks, and stay motivated and focused on your goals.

To build self-belief, it is essential to develop a growth mindset, embrace challenges, and cultivate a positive self-image. You can also build self-belief by visualizing your success, using positive affirmations, and focusing on your strengths and achievements.

Self-motivation is the drive to achieve your goals and fulfill your dreams. It is the ability to stay focused, disciplined, and committed to your aspirations, even in the face of challenges and setbacks. Self-motivation allows you to overcome procrastination, self-doubt, and fear of failure and to take consistent action towards your goals.

To build self-motivation, it is essential to set clear goals, create a plan of action, and maintain a positive attitude. You can also build self-motivation by seeking inspiration and motivation from others, staying organized and disciplined, and rewarding yourself for your achievements.

28: SELF-EMPOWERMENT: TAKING CHARGE OF YOUR LIFE AND MAKING POSITIVE CHANGES

In conclusion, self-empowerment is about taking charge of your life and creating the life you want. It requires self-awareness, self-confidence, self-belief, and self-motivation. By cultivating these qualities and practicing the strategies and tips outlined in this chapter, you can unlock your true potential and achieve your goals. Remember, self-empowerment is not a one-time event but a lifelong journey of personal growth and transformation. So, embrace the process, stay committed, and believe in yourself, and you will create a fulfilling life in the modern world.

29: Self-Leadership: How to Lead Yourself to Success

Self-Leadership: How to Lead Yourself to Success

Introduction

Self-leadership is the foundation of personal growth and success. It is the ability to take control of your own life and lead yourself in the direction of your dreams and aspirations. In this chapter, we will explore what self-leadership is, why it is important, and how you can develop it to achieve your goals.

What is Self-Leadership?

Self-leadership is the process of taking responsibility for your own life and directing it towards your desired outcomes. It involves being self-aware, self-motivated, and self-disciplined. Self-leadership is the ability to manage your own emotions, thoughts, and actions in a way that aligns with your goals and values.

Why is Self-Leadership Important?

Self-leadership is important because it enables you to take

control of your life and make the most of your potential. It helps you to be proactive, rather than reactive, in your approach to life. Self-leadership allows you to develop resilience and adaptability, which are essential qualities for success in today's fast-paced and constantly changing world.

How to Develop Self-Leadership?

Developing self-leadership requires a conscious effort to cultivate certain qualities and skills. Here are some ways you can develop self-leadership:

Develop Self-Awareness

Self-awareness is the foundation of self-leadership. It involves being aware of your strengths, weaknesses, values, beliefs, and emotions. To develop self-awareness, take time to reflect on your thoughts and feelings. Journaling, mindfulness practices, and seeking feedback from others can help you to develop self-awareness.

Set Clear Goals

Setting clear goals is essential for self-leadership. Goals provide direction and focus, and help you to prioritize your actions. Make sure your goals are specific, measurable, achievable, relevant, and time-bound (SMART). Write your goals down and revisit them regularly to stay focused and motivated.

Develop Self-Motivation

Self-motivation is the ability to drive yourself towards your goals, even when faced with challenges and obstacles. To develop self-motivation, identify your sources of motivation, such as your values, passions, or sense of purpose. Visualize your desired outcomes and imagine how achieving your goals will benefit you and others.

Cultivate Self-Discipline

Self-discipline is the ability to stick to your goals and commitments, even when it's difficult. To develop self-discipline, create a routine and stick to it. Use positive self-talk to motivate yourself and avoid procrastination. Practice delayed gratification by prioritizing long-term goals over short-term pleasures.

Develop Resilience

Resilience is the ability to bounce back from setbacks and challenges. To develop resilience, reframe challenges as opportunities for growth and learning. Practice self-compassion and forgiveness, and seek support from others when needed. Focus on your strengths and accomplishments, and learn from your failures and mistakes.

Practice Self-Care

Self-care is essential for self-leadership. It involves taking care of your physical, emotional, and mental well-being. To practice self-care, prioritize sleep, exercise, healthy eating, and stress management. Take breaks when needed and engage in activities that bring you joy and fulfillment.

Conclusion

Self-leadership is the foundation of personal growth and success. It is the ability to take control of your own life and lead yourself in the direction of your dreams and aspirations. Developing self-leadership requires a conscious effort to cultivate self-awareness, set clear goals, develop self-motivation and self-discipline, cultivate resilience, and practice self-care. By developing these qualities and skills, you can unlock your true potential and live a fulfilling life in the modern world.

Self-leadership is not a one-time task; it requires consistent effort and practice. It's a lifelong journey that requires you to continuously learn and grow. By developing self-leadership, you will be better equipped to navigate the complexities of modern life and achieve your goals.

Self-leadership is also a fundamental skill for leadership. As a leader, you must first lead yourself before you can lead others effectively. By developing self-leadership, you will become a better leader, able to inspire and motivate others towards a common goal.

In conclusion, self-leadership is a critical skill for personal growth and success. It involves taking responsibility for your own life, developing self-awareness, setting clear goals, cultivating self-motivation and self-discipline, cultivating resilience, and practicing self-care. By developing self-leadership, you can unlock your true potential and lead a fulfilling life in the modern world.

30: Self-Reflection and Personal Development: A Lifelong Journey

Introduction:

Self-reflection is an essential tool for personal development and self-awareness. It is the process of looking inward to examine our thoughts, feelings, and behaviors to gain a better understanding of ourselves. Self-reflection helps us identify our strengths and weaknesses, recognize patterns in our behavior, and gain insights into our motivations and values. By developing a regular self-reflection practice, we can take control of our lives, make better decisions, and live a more fulfilling life. In this chapter, we will explore the benefits of self-reflection, the different methods of self-reflection, and how to make self-reflection a lifelong practice.

The Benefits of Self-Reflection:

Self-reflection offers a range of benefits that can improve our lives. Here are some of the benefits of self-reflection:

Increased self-awareness: By reflecting on our thoughts, feelings, and behaviors, we can gain a better understanding of ourselves. This can help us identify our strengths and weaknesses and make better decisions.

Better decision-making: Self-reflection can help us make better decisions by providing us with insights into our motivations and values. This can help us align our actions with our goals and values.

Improved relationships: By understanding ourselves better, we can improve our relationships with others. We can develop better communication skills, become more empathetic, and build stronger connections with others.

Reduced stress and anxiety: Self-reflection can help us identify the sources of our stress and anxiety. By understanding the causes of our stress, we can take steps to reduce it.

Personal growth: Self-reflection is an essential tool for personal growth. By reflecting on our experiences, we can learn from our mistakes, develop new skills, and become better versions of ourselves.

Methods of Self-Reflection:

There are several different methods of self-reflection. Here are some of the most effective methods:

Journaling: Writing down our thoughts and feelings in a journal is an excellent way to reflect on our experiences. Journaling allows us to process our emotions and gain insights into our behaviors.

Meditation: Meditation is a powerful tool for self-reflection. By focusing our attention on our thoughts and feelings, we can gain a better understanding of ourselves.

Self-assessment tools: There are several self-assessment tools available, such as personality tests and values assessments, that can help us gain insights into our strengths and weaknesses.

Feedback from others: Receiving feedback from others can be a valuable tool for self-reflection. By listening to the perspectives of others, we can gain new insights into ourselves.

Making Self-Reflection a Lifelong Practice:

Self-reflection is not a one-time activity; it is a lifelong practice. Here are some tips for making self-reflection a regular part of your life:

30: SELF-REFLECTION AND PERSONAL DEVELOPMENT: A LIFELONG JOURNEY

Set aside time for self-reflection: Schedule time each day or week for self-reflection. Treat this time as an important appointment with yourself.

Make it a habit: Develop a routine for self-reflection. For example, you could journal every morning or meditate before bed.

Be honest with yourself: Self-reflection requires honesty and self-awareness. Be willing to examine your thoughts, feelings, and behaviors without judgment.

Be open to change: Self-reflection can be uncomfortable, but it can also lead to personal growth and transformation. Be open to changing your behavior and beliefs based on your reflections.

Seek support: Self-reflection can be challenging, and it is okay to seek support from others. Consider joining a support group or working with a therapist to help you through the process.

Conclusion:

Self-reflection is an essential tool for personal development and self-awareness. By regularly reflecting on our thoughts, feelings, and behaviors, we can gain a better understanding of ourselves, make better decisions, and live a more fulfilling life. The benefits of self-reflection are numerous, including increased self-awareness, improved decision-making, better relationships, reduced stress and anxiety, and personal growth.

There are several different methods of self-reflection, including journaling, meditation, self-assessment tools, and feedback from others. Each method has its advantages, and it's up to each individual to find the method that works best for them.

Making self-reflection a lifelong practice requires dedication, honesty, and openness to change. It's essential to set aside time for self-reflection, make it a habit, be honest with ourselves, be open to change, and seek support when needed.

Self-reflection is not always easy, but it is worth the effort. By developing a regular self-reflection practice, we can gain a deeper understanding of ourselves, make better decisions, and live a more fulfilling life. As we continue on our journey

of self-reflection and personal development, we may encounter challenges and setbacks, but with perseverance and
commitment, we can overcome them and continue to grow
and evolve.

31: The Role of Self-Awareness in Relationships: Improving Communication and Connection

Relationships are an essential part of our lives. We all have relationships with family members, friends, colleagues, romantic partners, and even strangers. These relationships can bring joy, fulfillment, and purpose to our lives. At the same time, they can also be a source of frustration, conflict, and stress. The quality of our relationships depends on many factors, including our communication skills, empathy, trust, and understanding of ourselves and others. In this chapter, we will explore the role of self-awareness in relationships and how it can help improve communication and connection.

Self-awareness is the foundation of personal growth and development. It is the ability to recognize and understand our thoughts, feelings, behaviors, and values. Self-awareness enables us to identify our strengths and weaknesses, our likes and dislikes, our fears and aspirations. It allows us to recognize patterns in our behavior and emotions and understand how they influence our relationships with others. In short, self-awareness is the key to knowing ourselves and others better.

One of the main benefits of self-awareness in relationships is improved communication. Communication is the foundation of any healthy relationship, whether it's a romantic partnership, a friendship, or a professional relationship. Good communication involves not only expressing oneself but also listening to and understanding others. Self-awareness helps us become better listeners and communicators by allowing us to recognize our biases, assumptions, and triggers.

When we are self-aware, we can identify our emotional triggers and the beliefs that underlie them. For example, if we get defensive when someone criticizes us, we can explore why we feel that way. Perhaps we have a deep-seated fear of failure or rejection that makes us defensive. By understanding this about ourselves, we can communicate more effectively with others. We can acknowledge our feelings without letting them get in the way of a productive conversation. We can also recognize when our emotions are getting the best of us and take a step back to calm down before continuing the discussion.

Self-awareness also helps us understand others better. When we are aware of our own biases and assumptions, we can recognize them in others. We can also be more empathetic and understanding of others' perspectives. We can recognize that everyone has their own unique experiences, beliefs, and values that influence their behavior. This understanding allows us to communicate more effectively with others and build stronger, more fulfilling relationships.

Another way that self-awareness can improve relationships is by helping us identify our needs and boundaries. When we know ourselves well, we can communicate our needs and boundaries clearly and assertively. This can prevent misunderstandings and resentment in relationships. For example, if we need alone time to recharge, we can communicate that to our partner or friends. If we have a boundary around certain topics, we can express that as well. By setting clear boundaries and communicating our needs, we can build more respectful and healthy relationships.

Self-awareness also helps us manage conflicts more effectively. Conflicts are a natural part of any relationship, and how we handle them can make or break the relationship.

31: THE ROLE OF SELF-AWARENESS IN RELATION-SHIPS: IMPROVING COMMUNICATION AND CONNEC-TION

When we are self-aware, we can recognize our own role in conflicts and take responsibility for our actions. We can also recognize when our emotions are getting in the way of resolving the conflict and take steps to calm down before continuing the discussion. Additionally, we can recognize the other person's perspective and be more empathetic and understanding. By approaching conflicts with self-awareness, we can find solutions that work for everyone involved and strengthen the relationship.

In conclusion, self-awareness is a crucial component of healthy relationships. It allows us to communicate more effectively, understand ourselves and others better, set clear boundaries, and manage conflicts more effectively. Developing self-awareness takes time and effort, but the benefits are well worth it. By becoming more self-aware, we can build stronger, more fulfilling relationships that bring us joy and fulfillment. Here are some practical tips for developing self-awareness in relationships:

Practice mindfulness. Mindfulness is the practice of paying attention to the present moment without judgment. When we practice mindfulness, we become more aware of our thoughts, feelings, and bodily sensations. This awareness can help us recognize our triggers and emotional patterns in relationships.

Journaling. Journaling is a great way to reflect on our experiences, emotions, and behaviors. By writing down our thoughts and feelings, we can gain insight into our patterns and triggers. We can also identify areas for personal growth and development.

Seek feedback. Asking for feedback from others can be a powerful tool for developing self-awareness. When we ask for feedback, we open ourselves up to learning from others' perspectives. We can also gain insight into how others perceive us and how our behaviors impact others.

Take responsibility for your actions. When we take responsibility for our actions, we empower ourselves to make positive changes. It's important to recognize that we have control over our behavior and how we show up in relationships.

Practice self-compassion. Self-compassion is the practice of treating ourselves with kindness, care, and understanding.

31: THE ROLE OF SELF-AWARENESS IN RELATION-SHIPS: IMPROVING COMMUNICATION AND CONNEC-TION

When we practice self-compassion, we can be more forgiving and understanding of our own mistakes and shortcomings. This self-compassion can also extend to our relationships with others, helping us be more empathetic and understanding.

By developing self-awareness in relationships, we can improve our communication, deepen our connections, and create more fulfilling relationships. It takes time and effort, but the benefits are well worth it. So, take the time to reflect on your thoughts, feelings, and behaviors in relationships. Practice mindfulness, seek feedback, take responsibility for your actions, and practice self-compassion. With these tools, you can unlock your true potential for personal growth and transformation in your relationships.

32: Self-Awareness and Emotional Intelligence: How They Work Together

Self-awareness and emotional intelligence are two critical components of personal growth and development. In this chapter, we will explore the interrelationship between these two essential factors and how they can be used to enhance your life and relationships.

Self-awareness refers to the ability to understand one's emotions, thoughts, and behaviors. It involves being introspective and self-reflective, recognizing your strengths and weaknesses, and understanding how your actions impact yourself and others. On the other hand, emotional intelligence is the ability to recognize, understand, and manage your own emotions, as well as those of others. It involves being empathetic, recognizing social cues, and effectively communicating with others.

Self-awareness and emotional intelligence are interrelated in that self-awareness is the foundation for developing emotional intelligence. Without self-awareness, it is challenging to recognize and understand your emotions and how they impact your thoughts and behaviors. This lack of understanding can lead to poor decision-making, negative relationships, and a lack of personal growth.

Emotional intelligence, on the other hand, is the next step in the process of personal growth and development. Once you have developed a strong sense of self-awareness, you can begin to focus on developing emotional intelligence. Emotional intelligence is all about understanding and managing your emotions, as well as those of others. It involves being aware of your emotional state and recognizing how your emotions impact your interactions with others.

One of the most significant benefits of developing emotional intelligence is that it allows you to be more empathetic. Empathy is the ability to understand and share the feelings of others. By being empathetic, you can develop stronger relationships with others and improve your communication skills. You will be better able to understand the perspectives of others, which can help you resolve conflicts and build stronger relationships.

Developing emotional intelligence also involves recognizing social cues. This is particularly important in today's fast-paced, digital world, where communication often takes place online. Social cues can include tone of voice, body language, and facial expressions. By recognizing these cues, you can better understand the intent behind someone's communication and respond appropriately.

Effective communication is another critical aspect of emotional intelligence. Communication is the key to building strong relationships, and emotional intelligence plays a significant role in ensuring that communication is effective. Effective communication involves not only expressing your own thoughts and feelings but also actively listening to others. By actively listening, you can better understand the perspectives of others and respond in a way that is appropriate and empathetic.

Finally, developing emotional intelligence can help you manage stress and other negative emotions. By understanding and managing your emotions, you can avoid getting overwhelmed by stress and other negative feelings. Instead, you can focus on developing strategies to manage these emotions effectively and maintain a positive outlook on life.

In conclusion, self-awareness and emotional intelligence

are two critical components of personal growth and development. Self-awareness is the foundation for developing emotional intelligence, and emotional intelligence allows you to better understand and manage your emotions, as well as those of others. By developing these skills, you can improve your relationships, communication skills, and overall well-being.

33: Self-Awareness and Resilience: Strategies for Coping with Life's Challenges

Life is full of challenges, and it is not always easy to navigate them. We all face setbacks, failures, disappointments, and losses at some point in our lives, and these experiences can be overwhelming and demotivating. However, the ability to cope with these challenges and bounce back from adversity is what separates successful and happy people from those who struggle to find fulfillment and purpose in their lives.

In this chapter, we will explore the relationship between self-awareness and resilience and share practical strategies for developing these essential life skills.

What is Self-Awareness?

Self-awareness is the ability to recognize and understand your thoughts, feelings, and behaviors, and how they impact your life and the lives of those around you. It is a critical component of emotional intelligence and a foundation for personal growth and development.

Self-awareness allows you to identify your strengths and

weaknesses, understand your values and beliefs, and recognize patterns in your behavior and relationships. It enables you to make informed decisions, manage your emotions, and communicate effectively with others.

Why is Self-Awareness Important for Resilience?

Resilience is the ability to adapt to change, overcome obstacles, and bounce back from adversity. It is a skill that can be developed and strengthened over time, but it requires self-awareness to be effective.

When you are self-aware, you are better equipped to cope with life's challenges because you have a deeper understanding of your strengths and weaknesses. You are more likely to recognize when you need help, and you are better able to communicate your needs to others.

Self-awareness also allows you to manage your emotions and stay focused on your goals, even when you face setbacks and failures. It enables you to take responsibility for your actions and make positive changes to improve your life.

Strategies for Developing Self-Awareness and Resilience

33: SELF-AWARENESS AND RESILIENCE: STRATEGIES FOR COPING WITH LIFE'S CHALLENGES

Practice Mindfulness

Mindfulness is the practice of being present in the moment and paying attention to your thoughts, feelings, and surroundings without judgment. It is a powerful tool for developing self-awareness and managing your emotions.

Start by setting aside a few minutes each day to practice mindfulness. Sit in a quiet place, close your eyes, and focus on your breath. When your mind wanders, gently bring your attention back to your breath. Over time, you will become more aware of your thoughts and feelings and better able to manage them.

Reflect on Your Values and Beliefs

Your values and beliefs shape your thoughts, feelings, and behavior. Take some time to reflect on what is most important to you and how your values and beliefs impact your life.

Write down your values and beliefs and reflect on how they align with your goals and aspirations. Are there any areas where your values and beliefs conflict with your goals? How can you reconcile these conflicts to create a more fulfilling life?

Set Realistic Goals

Setting goals is essential for personal growth and development, but it is also important to set realistic goals that align with your values and strengths. When you set unrealistic goals, you set yourself up for failure, which can be demotivating and discouraging.

Start by setting small, achievable goals that build on your strengths and align with your values. As you achieve these goals, you will build confidence and resilience, which will enable you to tackle more significant challenges.

Build a Support Network

No one can face life's challenges alone. Building a support network of friends, family, and mentors can help you navigate difficult times and stay focused on your goals.

Reach out to people who share your values and interests and who can offer encouragement and support. Join a community group, volunteer organization, or social club to meet new people and build meaningful connections.

Practice Self-Care

Self-care is essential for maintaining good physical and mental health. It includes activities such as exercise, healthy eating, adequate sleep, and relaxation techniques.

Make self-care a priority in your daily routine. Set aside time for exercise, meditation, or other activities that help you relax and recharge. Practice good sleep hygiene by sticking to a regular sleep schedule and creating a sleep-conducive environment.

Embrace Failure

Failure is a natural part of life, and it is essential to learn how to embrace it and use it as a learning opportunity. When you fail, reflect on what went wrong and what you can do differently next time.

Rather than dwelling on your mistakes, focus on the lessons learned and how you can use that knowledge to grow and improve. Celebrate your successes, no matter how small, and use them to build confidence and resilience.

Cultivate a Positive Mindset

33: SELF-AWARENESS AND RESILIENCE: STRATEGIES FOR COPING WITH LIFE'S CHALLENGES

A positive mindset is a powerful tool for resilience. When you have a positive attitude, you are more likely to see challenges as opportunities for growth and development.

Practice reframing negative thoughts into positive ones. For example, instead of saying "I can't do this," try saying "I haven't figured this out yet, but I will keep trying." Surround yourself with positive people and positive experiences that uplift and inspire you.

Conclusion

Self-awareness and resilience are essential life skills that can help you navigate life's challenges and achieve your goals. By practicing mindfulness, reflecting on your values and beliefs, setting realistic goals, building a support network, practicing self-care, embracing failure, and cultivating a positive mindset, you can develop these skills and unlock your true potential.

Remember, developing self-awareness and resilience is a journey, not a destination. It takes time, effort, and patience, but the rewards are worth it. With practice and perseverance, you can build a fulfilling life that is resilient to

33: SELF-AWARENESS AND RESILIENCE: STRATEGIES FOR COPING WITH LIFE'S CHALLENGES

the challenges and setbacks that come your way.

34: Self-Awareness and Mindset: The Power of Positive Thinking

Introduction

Your mindset is the foundation upon which your life is built. It determines your attitude, your actions, and ultimately your success. Developing a positive mindset is a crucial step in the journey towards self-awareness and personal growth. In this chapter, we will explore the power of positive thinking and how it can transform your life for the better.

The Power of Your Mindset

Your mindset is the lens through which you see the world. It shapes your perceptions, attitudes, and behaviors. A positive mindset can help you overcome challenges, find opportunities, and achieve your goals. On the other hand, a negative mindset can hold you back, make you feel stuck, and limit your potential.

Research has shown that our thoughts and beliefs have a significant impact on our physical and emotional well-being. Negative thoughts and beliefs can lead to stress, anxiety, and even depression. In contrast, positive thoughts and beliefs can improve our mood, reduce stress, and boost our immune system.

The Power of Positive Thinking

Positive thinking is the practice of focusing on the good in any situation, even when faced with challenges. It's about seeing the glass as half full rather than half empty. Positive thinking does not mean ignoring problems or pretending everything is okay when it's not. Instead, it's about approaching challenges with a solution-oriented mindset, and finding ways to overcome them.

Positive thinking has been linked to a range of benefits, including:

Increased resilience: Positive thinkers are better equipped to handle setbacks and bounce back from adversity.

Improved relationships: Positive people are more attractive to others, and tend to have more fulfilling relationships.

Better physical health: Positive people are less likely to suffer from stress-related illnesses such as heart disease, high blood pressure, and diabetes.

Increased success: Positive thinkers are more likely to achieve their goals and succeed in life.

Changing Your Mindset

Developing a positive mindset is not always easy, especially if you have a tendency towards negative thinking. However, with practice and perseverance, it is possible to change your mindset and transform your life. Here are some tips for developing a more positive mindset:

Practice gratitude: Take time each day to focus on the things you are grateful for. This can be as simple as appreciating the sunshine, or as profound as being thankful for your health or your loved ones. Cultivating an attitude of gratitude can help shift your focus towards the positive aspects of your life.

Reframe negative thoughts: When you catch yourself thinking negatively, try to reframe the thought in a more positive light. For example, instead of thinking "I can't do this," try thinking "I haven't figured this out yet, but I'm making progress." Reframing negative thoughts can help you see challenges as opportunities for growth, rather than insurmountable obstacles.

Surround yourself with positivity: Spend time with people who lift you up and inspire you. Avoid negative people who bring you down or drain your energy. Seek out positive role models who embody the qualities and values you admire.

Practice self-care: Taking care of yourself physically, emotionally, and spiritually can help you maintain a positive mindset. This might include exercise, meditation, spending time in nature, or engaging in creative hobbies.

Conclusion

Developing a positive mindset is an essential part of self-awareness and personal growth. By cultivating a positive outlook, you can overcome challenges, achieve your goals, and live a more fulfilling life. Remember that changing your mindset is a process that takes time and effort, but the rewards are well worth it. With practice and perseverance, you can unlock the power of positive thinking and transform your life for the better.

35: Self-Awareness and Authenticity: Being True to Yourself in a World of Expectations

Introduction

Self-awareness is the foundation of personal growth and transformation. It is the ability to observe, understand, and accept our thoughts, emotions, and behavior. When we are self-aware, we can identify our strengths and weaknesses, recognize our patterns and triggers, and make conscious choices that align with our values and goals. Self-awareness is not just about introspection, but also about seeking feedback, learning from experiences, and developing empathy for others. In this chapter, we will explore the connection between self-awareness and authenticity, and how we can cultivate both in a world that often pressures us to conform to external expectations.

Authenticity: What Does It Mean to Be True to Yourself?

Authenticity is the quality of being genuine, honest, and transparent. It is about expressing yourself in a way that is true to your inner self, without fear of judgment or rejection. Authenticity is not about being perfect, but about embracing your imperfections and vulnerabilities. When we are authentic, we build trust and credibility with others, and we attract people who share our values and vision.

However, being true to ourselves is not always easy. We live in a society that often rewards conformity and punishes deviation. We are bombarded with social norms, cultural stereotypes, and media messages that tell us how we should look, think, and behave. We face pressure to fit in, to please others, and to maintain a certain image or status. As a result, we may hide our true selves, suppress our emotions, or engage in behaviors that do not align with our values.

The Importance of Self-Awareness in Authenticity

To be authentic, we need to know ourselves first. We need to understand our beliefs, needs, and desires, and how they shape our thoughts and actions. We need to be aware of our strengths and weaknesses, and how they impact our relationships and goals. We need to recognize our triggers and biases, and how they affect our perception of reality.

Self-awareness is the key to unlocking authenticity. When we are self-aware, we can make conscious choices that reflect our true selves, rather than being driven by external factors. We can set boundaries, say no, and stand up for our values without feeling guilty or ashamed. We can express our feelings and opinions in a respectful and assertive way, without fear of conflict or rejection. We can take risks, make mistakes, and learn from failures, without losing our sense of self-worth.

Cultivating Self-Awareness for Authenticity

Self-awareness is not a fixed trait, but a skill that can be developed and enhanced over time. Here are some practical ways to cultivate self-awareness for authenticity:

Practice mindfulness: Mindfulness is the practice of being present and non-judgmental in the moment. By paying attention to our thoughts, emotions, and sensations without reacting to them, we can develop a greater sense of self-awareness and inner peace. Mindfulness can be practiced through meditation, yoga, or simple breathing exercises.

Reflect on your values: Our values are the principles that guide our decisions and actions. Reflecting on our values can help us clarify our priorities, and make choices that align with our true selves. Make a list of your core values, and ask yourself how they show up in your daily life.

Seek feedback: Feedback from others can be a valuable source of insight and growth. Ask trusted friends or mentors for honest feedback on your strengths and weaknesses, and how you can improve. Be open to constructive criticism, and use it as a learning opportunity.

Keep a journal: Journaling is a powerful tool for self-reflection and self-expression. Write down your thoughts, feelings, and experiences, and reflect on how they relate to your goals and values. Use your journal as a safe space to explore your inner self, without fear of judgment or criticism.

Challenge your biases: We all have biases and assumptions that can cloud our judgment and limit our perspective. Challenge your biases by exposing yourself to diverse opinions, cultures, and experiences. Practice empathy by putting yourself in other people's shoes, and seeking to understand their point of view.

Practice self-compassion: Self-compassion is the practice of treating yourself with kindness, care, and understanding, especially in times of difficulty or failure. Be gentle with yourself, and avoid self-criticism or self-blame. Treat yourself as you would treat a dear friend.

Set boundaries: Setting boundaries is an important aspect of self-care and self-respect. Identify your limits and needs, and communicate them clearly and assertively to others. Say no when you need to, and prioritize your own well-being.

Conclusion

Self-awareness and authenticity are two sides of the same coin. To be authentic, we need to be self-aware, and to be self-aware, we need to be authentic. By cultivating self-awareness, we can break free from external expectations, and live a life that is true to our inner selves. We can build meaningful relationships, pursue fulfilling careers, and make a positive impact on the world. Self-awareness is not a destination, but a journey that requires practice, patience, and perseverance. But the rewards of self-awareness are immeasurable, and can lead to a life of joy, purpose, and fulfillment.

36: Conclusion: The Importance of Self-Awareness for Living a Fulfilling Life

In this comprehensive guide, we have explored the topic of self-awareness and how it can help us to unlock our true potential and live a fulfilling life in the modern world. We have covered a range of topics, including the definition of self-awareness, the benefits of self-awareness, how to develop self-awareness, and how to use self-awareness to improve our lives.

We have learned that self-awareness is the ability to recognize and understand our thoughts, feelings, and behaviors. It is the foundation of personal growth and transformation, as it allows us to identify our strengths and weaknesses, and to make positive changes in our lives.

We have also discovered that there are many benefits of self-awareness, including increased emotional intelligence, improved relationships, better decision-making, and greater resilience in the face of challenges. By developing self-awareness, we can become more effective leaders, better parents and partners, and happier, more fulfilled individuals.

To develop self-awareness, we have explored a range of techniques, including mindfulness meditation, journaling, and seeking feedback from others. These techniques can help us to become more aware of our thoughts, emotions, and behaviors, and to identify patterns and habits that may be holding us back.

We have also learned that self-awareness is not a one-time achievement, but an ongoing process that requires constant attention and effort. By continually practicing self-awareness, we can deepen our understanding of ourselves and others, and continue to grow and evolve as individuals.

Finally, we have discussed how to use self-awareness to improve our lives, including setting goals, developing healthy habits, and cultivating positive relationships. By using self-awareness as a tool for personal growth and transformation, we can create the life we truly want and achieve our full potential.

In conclusion, self-awareness is a powerful tool that can help us to unlock our true potential and live a fulfilling life

36: CONCLUSION: THE IMPORTANCE OF SELF-AWARENESS FOR LIVING A FULFILLING LIFE

in the modern world. By developing self-awareness and using it as a tool for personal growth and transformation, we can become happier, healthier, and more fulfilled individuals. So take the time to develop your self-awareness, and start living the life you truly want today!

Thank You

As we reach the end of this book, I want to say thanks for reading this book.

I want to get this information out to as many people as possible. If you found this book helpful, I would greatly appreciate you leaving me a review. This helps others find the book as well.

Disclaimer

This document is geared towards providing exact and reliable information in regards to the topic and issue covered. The publication is sold on the idea that the publisher is not required to render an accounting, officially permitted, or otherwise, qualified services. If advice is necessary, legal, financial, medical or professional, a practiced individual in the profession should be ordered.

This information is not presented by a financial or medical practitioner and is for entertainment, educational and informational purposes only. The content is not intended as a substitute for professional medical advice, diagnosis, or treatment. Always seek the advice of your physician or other qualified health care provider with any questions you may have regarding a medical condition. Never disregard professional medical advice or delay in seeking it because of something you have read.

The information provided herein is stated to be truthful and consistent, in that any liability, in terms of inattention or otherwise, by any usage or abuse of any policies, processes, or directions contained within is the solitary and utter responsibility of the recipient reader. Under no circumstances

DISCLAIMER

will any legal responsibility or blame be held against the publisher for any reparation, damages, or monetary loss due to the information herein, either directly or indirectly.